If Not Now, When?

If Not Now, When?
Living the Baby Boomer Adventure

Esther Rantzen

headline
springboard

First published in 2008
by HEADLINE SPRINGBOARD

An imprint of Headline Publishing Group

1

Cataloguing in Publication Data is available from the British Library

ISBN 978 0 7553 1719 6

Typeset in Perpetua by Avon DataSet Ltd, Bidford on Avon, Warwickshire

Printed and bound in Great Britain by
Clays Ltd, St Ives plc

Headline's policy is to use papers that are natural, renewable and recyclable
products and made from wood grown in sustainable forests. The logging and
manufacturing processes are expected to conform to the environmental
regulations of the country of origin.

HEADLINE PUBLISHING GROUP
An Hachette Livre UK Company
338 Euston Road
London NW1 3BH

www.headline.co.uk
www.hachettelivre.co.uk

To my sister, Scilla Taylor, in gratitude for
her wisdom, wit and intuition, and in admiration
for her commitment and courage.

Acknowledgements

I first explored some of these thoughts in the *Daily Mail*, and I would particularly like to thank the Features and the Femail teams who are mischievous, perceptive, and a pleasure to work with. My agent, Luigi Bonomi, is a dear friend, and I greatly value his laughter, his generosity and his unfailing confidence in me. My publisher, Val Hudson, is strong, clever and stylish, as well as being brilliant at her job. Her patient, diligent assistant Philippa Hobbs has been a constant support. And there are literally hundreds of baby boomers who have offered me advice, encouragement and allowed me to write about their experiences. Some I have disguised to spare their blushes, so to them I say, if you think you recognize yourself in these pages, I assure you, it must be someone else. And to Bryher Scudamore, John Pitman, Mike Bowen, Jan Kennedy, Vicki Mellor, Kate Cymerman and all the friends, family and colleagues who have enriched my baby-boomer years, I say thank you. If luck is on our side I look forward enormously to spending the next three or four decades with you, and enjoying yet more adventures together.

Contents

Chapter One

Why the Baby Boomers are Having the Time of their Lives

> *I can remember when the air was clean and the sex dirty*

George Burns

I once had to walk the streets for a living, asking people for their opinions on life, living and the issues of the day. I was a television interviewer, and my quest was for people with lively minds, a sense of humour and vitality, who would make our viewers think and laugh. I rapidly discovered as I walked through the villages, town and cities of Britain that youngsters were no good for my purpose. They were too self-conscious: if I asked them a question they either giggled, or ran away. The middle-aged were no better: they were too self-important and busy to stop for me, and if I tried to pursue them, they strode on, heads down, frowning.

So I concentrated on the over-sixties, who had time to talk to me, and were guaranteed to tell me exactly what they thought, without fear or favour. They had opinions on every subject, and if other people disagreed, so much the worse for them. Why should they care what anyone else thought? They were original and entertaining, and our viewers loved them. In fact, we interviewed them so often on my weekly programme for consumers, *That's Life!* that we created stars overnight; one in particular, Annie Mizen, was well over eighty when she began her new career as a television pundit, opening fêtes and giving autographs. The point about the older people I met is that although I don't suppose they were rich materially, they had amassed a treasure-trove of experience, and they had learned over the years how to enjoy life, and what to prioritise. They put love, laughter and a sense of adventure at the top of the list. They had independent minds, because over the years they had discovered their opinions were as good as anyone else's, and they were unafraid of looking foolish, because they knew that even the finest minds make the stupidest mistakes. My father, a distinguished mathematician and physicist, taught me that.

He rarely went out with matching socks. So when the sun shone and I stood in front of my over-sixties with a camera and a microphone they stopped, listened, and gave me an entertaining piece of their minds.

They are still with us, the older people with so much to say – in fact there are more of them than ever, and yet it seems that, these days, nobody is listening. Our media are almost exclusively dominated by the under-forties, and when you do catch a glimpse of an elderly man or woman, they are almost invariably portrayed as a victim, suffering illness, abuse or neglect. Economically, the grey pound is powerful and plentiful: these are the buyers of music, entertainment, long-haul holidays, and quality consumer goods. And yet if they feature at all in advertisements, it will be for stair-lifts or incontinence pads. No wonder our young dread growing older. What have they got to look forward to? But the truth is that, with a little luck, reasonable health and enough savings not to have to grind along watching every penny, they should be looking forward to the time of their lives. After all, the 'third age' is the chance to become yourself again. Gone are the years of anxiety and ambition, when you have to fulfil so many arduous roles: bread-winner, parent, educator, cook, gardener, chauffeur, painter and decorator, and so much else. Gone are the years when you went without sleep, when you didn't have time to read a book or have a meal with friends, when the loo was the only place you could ever be alone. Now you can rediscover yourself and indulge the dreams you had long forgotten.

In your youth, did you fantasise about travel? Or getting a degree? Or learning to ballroom dance? So did I, and in my late sixties those dreams have unexpectedly come true. We oldies, it seems, have ambitions that have been maturing over the years, like fine wine, and now is the time, as Shirley Bassey put it, to pop our corks. A recent survey of a thousand over-sixties revealed that comfy slippers and snoozing by the fireside came nowhere in their plans. They were determined to take up parachuting and hang-gliding, to see the Northern Lights and swim with dolphins, to go to the opera, grow a beard and have more sex. Not what you might call opting for the quiet life. Why have older people such a highly developed sense of adventure? Because being over sixty concentrates the mind wonderfully. Age has its price. At twenty we thought we would live for ever, and so would our friends and family. Now, as some of those closest to us are taken from us, we become very aware of our own mortality. Time is precious, and not to be wasted. But that knowledge doesn't mean we have to wrap ourselves in cotton-wool. Quite the reverse. Now is the time to take a few risks. Why ever not? After all, hard experience has taught us that life and death are completely unpredictable. Every time we take a car journey or eat a kebab we risk accident or illness, and who knows when the earth will collide with an asteroid. To put it brutally, if none of us knows how much time we have left, that knowledge should make up our minds for us. When opportunity comes our way, we must ask ourselves, in Rabbi Hillel's famous phrase, 'If not now, when?' And the answer for most of us, the 'baby boomers', is now.

Chapter Two

Money

> *And I shall spend my pension on*
> *brandy and summer gloves . . .*
>
> Jenny Joseph, 'Warning'

Just a moment! Suddenly it feels as if the blade of the guillotine is swishing a bit too close to our necks. Does old age really mean we have to live entirely on our pensions, and stop earning altogether? Surely not. As long as we have our health and strength, and want to work, why shouldn't we? Some of us may prefer to retire completely, may relish the freedom to jump off the conveyor belt or break away from the coal face. Others may hate the idea of hours with nothing to do, and nowhere to go. The good news is that there is, or should be, an element of choice here. Now that it's against the law to discriminate against people on the grounds of their age, everyone is having to rethink the concept of a fixed 'retirement age'. Employers aren't nearly so keen to dump their older workers into the nearest garbage can. Indeed, big companies, like WH Smith and Sainsbury's, and industries like garden centres and DIY stores are discovering that older workers are a valuable resource. Every now and then newspapers print scary headlines about old people being 'forced' to work well past retirement age. That wouldn't scare me at all. On the contrary, I would be horrified if anyone tried to prevent me working until I drop. Not perhaps scurrying to the office and spending all day and every day there, as I did in my mad, workaholic youth, but certainly having enough work to give me a feeling of achievement at the end of the week, and a team to work alongside. For people who feel the way I do, it may well be that we have more to spend on brandy than simply our pensions.

However, many people don't have that choice. It takes loads of luck to continue working all through our seventies and eighties – we must be physically and mentally up to it, and be given the opportunity. Whether we are still working, or retire, for all of us the third age is a time when we wonder how best to plan our finances for the future. There is no single answer that fits every case, of course. And, anyway, this is not a 'how to get rich, stay rich and make sure your nearest and dearest get some of your riches' advice book. Sadly, I do not possess a crystal ball I can use to beam into the money markets of the future, and nobody else has either. Financial forecasting is like weather forecasting with a piece of seaweed, only without the seaweed. Yes, I suppose the hugely rich are protected against possible disaster in the stock market, the property market and the banks, but then again, history is full of mighty tycoons who have come crashing to the ground. Just think of all those lords of the manor who had to sell their grand homes because they couldn't afford to mend the roof. And then, of course, there's inheritance tax. But we'll come to that later. Experts I have consulted over the years tell me that if you want to weather unpredictable storms, the trick is to save as much as you can, then put your nest egg in three places; cash, the stock market and property. That way, whatever crashes and burns, and we have lived long enough to know that anything can, some of your hard-earned cash must surely be safe.

But, of course, even the best experts can be wrong. They tell us we must make sure we save for a rainy day because old age can be the most expensive time of our lives. And yet my late husband Desmond Wilcox, the brilliant documentary film-maker, at the age of sixty in a moment of madness blew the whole of his pension the moment it matured on a round-the-world trip for the family. That turned out to be the best decision he made, because, alas, Desi died far too young, at sixty-nine. What good would that pension have done him if the lump sum had stayed in the bank, accruing interest? Just imagine if, instead of the glorious memories that my children and I prize so highly of the Taj Mahal and Bali, we had a few extra pounds in the bank? There's no comparison. Then there's the fact that you and I probably belong to the generation that considers concentration on money at best materialistic and at worst plain greedy. In my respectable home, in the suburbs of London where I grew up just after the Second World War, three subjects were considered too vulgar to discuss around a polite dinner table: food, vanity and money.

Let me digress a little. Although I find the subject of how to pile up loads of money a bit on the dull side, I'm aware this is a fault in me. Certainly, failing to take an interest in the food we eat is the British fatal flaw. We have wonderful countryside, unrivalled architecture, we excel at poetry, drama, painting, and some of our music isn't bad, but our ghastly cooking is renowned around the world. Don't tell me we've changed for the better over the years. All we've done, in desperation, is import the skills of the French, the Italian, the Swiss and the Asian nations, all the kindly immigrants who have opened restaurants and trained our chefs. As I write, the television channels are crammed with cookery programmes. We watch, we salivate, and then we go out and buy ready-meals and takeaways. We get fatter and fatter, and cook less and less. I blame our native Puritanical streak, which insists that caring about what we eat is greedy and vulgar. Maybe we baby-boomers are the worst food Philistines because our British insensitivity to food was exacerbated by the stringencies of the Second World War. I was a toddler during the 1940s, brought up on a diet that now sounds very healthy but can't have been much fun. One egg a week, a scraping of butter, very little meat but loads of fish, tablespoons each night filled with extract of malt, rose-hip syrup and cod liver oil. I got good at holding my nose to stifle the taste.

During the war, my family lived in the country, kept chickens and pickled their eggs in great big bowls, but when we took them out to eat them, they never looked like the warm, brown fresh eggs we had collected from our hens. When our apples ripened and fell, we would gather them up and wrap them in newspaper, from which they would emerge throughout the winter wrinkled and unappetising. I remember eating junket sprinkled with nutmeg. Again, I'm sure it was good for me, but the sour taste lingers on my tongue. If all that natural, low-fat, additive-free food bred strong bones and lowered my cholesterol, it did nothing to educate my tastebuds.

My family even took an odd pride in not enjoying food. 'Some people,' my father used to say scornfully, 'live to eat. We eat to live.' My mother learned to cook after she got married, and my father's loftiness led her into strange habits. Once she had mastered a dish, like baked apples, she would cook it for us every week. I never much cared for baked apples in the first place and no matter how often she served them, those sad apples never improved. The core was prickly and the flesh was mushy, but true to the family tradition, I didn't feel I could comment. That would have been ill-mannered. And even to notice what we were eating, or leaving on the side of our plates, was vulgar.

Vanity was off-limits, too. My father used to say, with a bewildered smile, 'The moment we brought a mirror into the house, my daughters lost the capacity for thought.' If I make him sound like a Victorian dragon, I do him a great injustice. He was funny and absent-minded (hence the odd socks), but he had grown up with two brothers, so girls were a mystery to him. Indeed, looking at children today, when eating disorders are rampant and lookism reigns, we were lucky, in a way. There was no pressure at home for us to be pretty, or sexy, or catch a good husband. My sister and I were brought up like boys, in the sense that both our parents were vigilant about our schooling and determined we should go to university, then have a worthwhile career. In this, we were unusual among our contemporaries. Bear in mind that in most homes in the 1940s and 1950s, girls weren't expected to have an academic career: they were supposed to get married, have babies, and not rock the boat. When my school-friends were teenagers, they joyfully painted their lips bright red, tightened narrow little belts around their waists, put on the pointed bras and stiletto heels that were the trademark of the fifties, and flounced around in enormous skirts with stiff petticoats. I had nothing to put inside my bras, couldn't find my waist, but obediently bought myself an enormous green dress with rustling petticoats. I could hardly reach over it to the mirror in our hall to put on my lipstick, but whenever I tried, Dad would snort derisively, and make his remark about brains going out of the window. So I got the clear message that vanity, like food, was vulgar. Most vulgar of all was any desire or yearning for money. Neat, not gaudy, was the criterion. Money, like food, was a useful fuel, not to be spilled or splashed about. But, then, we never had enough to splash. We weren't poor – we had shoes on our feet and could pay the heating bill – but we certainly weren't rich. In 1945, when peace returned, we moved back into London where my parents had been living before the war. They found a little semi-detached mock-Tudor brick house in Cricklewood, a suburb in the north-west of the city. It had a small, rectangular back garden with flowerbeds lining a lawn; it was filled with bees, butterflies, lupins and hollyhocks in the summer, and our front garden was surrounded by the obligatory privet hedge. I wonder whether 'privet' is related to 'private', because that was its function, to mark the boundaries and ensure we kept ourselves to ourselves. That hedge required constant maintenance. I've never seen a privet tree, but had it ever been left to express itself, I'm sure our hedge could have grown into a wild privet forest. That never happened: it would have been blasphemy to our neighbourhood. Every Sunday Dad, like everyone else in the estate, was in our drive clipping away with his secateurs, keeping the hedge in its place. That is the scent of the suburbs to me, those dense green privet leaves hiding inconspicuous white flowers that smelt pungently like cat pee.

At the other end of the road were far bigger detached houses with grand mock-Georgian windows, and two cars in each drive. Just occasionally I would go to a birthday party in one of those homes, and notice the big hall, the acres of parquet floor and french windows. But I never envied my friends their mansions, and I came home from them with relief. I liked our neat, orderly lack of splendour. I never realised that we were sometimes bobbing a little too close to the waterline. Looking back, I now know there were times when my parents were anxious about money. My father came home one day to find Mum had bought a box of French marigolds for a few pennies for the front garden, and he flew into a rage. She called it 'pauperitis,' and told me he sometimes had nightmares about poverty. At the time he was head of the BBC's Engineering Designs Department, a prestigious job for a very talented scientist, but still my parents had to scrape his salary together to afford our holidays in B-and-Bs by the seaside.

I remember those holiday dinner-time puddings of

Spotted Dick, the name our landladies gave to steamed sponge studded with sultanas, and our afternoons on wind-swept beaches where Dad taught us to build real sandcastles with moats. My friends might have taken more luxurious holidays in hotels or even abroad, but who cared? We were happy.

Prudence had been bred into us. So that, I suppose, is why I and so many of my age group find the whole approach to money as the point of life and living, and conspicuous consumption as being the ideal lifestyle, all unbearably vulgar. When Desi and I developed successful television careers, with decent salaries, I remember him making a delicious glass of Pimm's for my mother as she sat watching the children swimming in our pool. She looked at me on the sun-bed next to her, and said, reflectively, 'This is all very *nouveau riche*.' She meant vulgar. You may have had a completely different childhood from mine. Perhaps you were brought up in a grand house, like the ones at the other end of our street, and were comparatively rich. (I say comparatively, because I have never met anyone of our generation who would admit to being really rich. Maybe the Sultan of Brunei does, but the rest will blush, look down, and admit to being 'comfortable'. Money, you see, is vulgar.) Maybe you had to contend with real poverty, like my uncle, whose mother used to make his shirts out of old sheets. Either way, rich or poor, in the third age we face the same dilemma: how best should we organise our money?

Let's hope you have a little more than the state pension to live on. If not, life can be pretty bleak. The major charities, like Age Concern and Help the Aged, which support and campaign for older people, have excellent publications designed to lead you through the jungle of regulations and entitlements. The only additional advice I can offer, if you're really skint, or even if you're not, is don't be too proud to explore your local charity shops. You'll be amazed how many people, not just the poor and the elderly, riffle through the racks of clothing and find the most amazing bargains. Yummy mummies do it all the time. I was alerted to this gold mine of wonderment by a television programme that asked me to try and dress well for a smart occasion by buying on a tight budget from my local charity shops, and I found a wonderful original Diane von Furstenberg wraparound dress for £25 which has become a real favourite. But life isn't filled with bargains. And although we now may be entitled to bus passes, and cheap seats on the trains and at cinemas, there's no escaping the fact that it's very, very difficult to live well on just the state pension. But when we conducted a survey for a BBC television programme about older people called *Never Too Late* we found that most people had a little something extra they had saved up, or a home they owned, so they weren't entirely dependent on the Chancellor's generosity. Even so, in our third age we usually face a declining income, and all too often the pension that may have sounded like glorious affluence when we first started paying our precious earnings into it has magically transformed itself into a sad little dribble of funds now we are old enough to use it. Should we spend whatever we have in the bank to eke out that declining income? What else should we do with our savings? How can we maintain a decent lifestyle, fulfil our dreams, yet have enough to cover eventualities such as full-time care? And when we finally pop our clogs, how best can we avoid our family having to pay a fortune to the Chancellor in inheritance tax?

Recently I came across an interesting answer to some of these problems: equity release. Basically that means borrowing money by selling off part of the value of your home on the condition that you can continue to live there. Of course you don't get the full value, and I know that in the 1990s there were tragic stories of people who had been cheated or found themselves deeply in debt as a result of some of the schemes that existed then. But since that time tough regulations have been brought in to protect you against getting into negative equity. Over the last couple of decades, property has increased so much in value that, for most of us, our home is by far our most valuable possession. On paper we may look rich. And yet if we sell up to try and use some of that money, we will still have to buy somewhere else to live in, and many of us are very emotionally attached to our family homes. Equity release would seem, for many people, to be the answer. It's the way we can release the money locked up in bricks and mortar, use it to improve our own quality of life, but still live in the home we love. Let me add two caveats. First, I should declare an interest. I have been employed by a company which offers information and advice about equity release. I agreed to act as their spokesperson because I investigated it thoroughly, and believe their advice can transform people's lives. The lump sum you get in return for a percentage of the value of your house can, if you wish, pay for a holiday, or for home improvements, or a new car, or private medical treatment. Furthermore, you can continue to live in your own home as long as you like. However, your heirs will no longer inherit the whole of your property. (They are unlikely to anyway, given the level at which inheritance tax kicks in, but don't get me started.) Will there be a family feud when they discover what you are considering? Possibly. But in my experience, however careful and fair you try to be when you write your will (and please do write your will, I can't believe how many people haven't), where there's a will there's a feud. The second caveat is that nobody knows whether the property boom will continue or fall into a black hole, and what your home will fetch when it is eventually sold. But that's where we began. There are, as we agreed at the start of this chapter, no crystal balls.

There is another way to release the money trapped in your bricks and mortar, if you have the courage. A friend of mine (a wonderful actor with whom, I'm sure, you've been in love for years, so have I, but discretion prevents me sharing his name with you) has persuaded his bank to let him take out an enormous overdraft, the total value of his house, which he owns outright. The interest is rolled up, so he never has to pay anything back until, on his death, the house is sold. His children will probably inherit nothing, but they don't care, and in any case he is giving them the money they need now, when they need it most, in his lifetime. He says his aim is not to leave a penny to anyone. He's not frightened about the size of the debt that is mounting up, minute by minute, even though, with compound interest, it will double every ten years, because he reckons that the value of his property will increase even faster. That, he thinks, will more than take care of the interest on the huge loan. Given that, at the time of writing, house prices are falling, he's much braver than I. Somehow I can't bring myself to follow his example. But he is happily travelling the world, playing golf on all the most glamorous courses around the Caribbean, and having a high old time. Good luck to him, and you, if you choose to follow his example. Whether you do or you don't, you can or you can't, his solution chimes with my view that now is the time to indulge your dreams. If not now, when? Let's assume that we have spent most of our youth and prime being careful and cautious. Let's also assume that all that time we thought flashing our money around and flaunting our income, modest though it may have been, by spending lavishly on ourselves was vulgar. Now is the time for vulgarity. SKIN! (Spend the Kids' Inheritance Now!) If you've always wanted to go to Machu Picchu, pack your bags and go. If you want to take a degree in antiques, for heaven's sake do it. (There is a wonderful degree course in antiques at Southampton Solent University. I gather one of their students was browsing in a market in East Anglia and found a Georgian diamond ring. That's another way to eke out your pension.)

Shouldn't you keep a little cash aside just in case you need that full-time carer in your declining years? Yes, I suppose you should. Otherwise you become a problem for the rest of your family. It won't be much fun for you or your children if they have to spend your last years worrying about your safety. How much should you put aside? Pass me that crystal ball. I can't guess – that's up to you to decide. Even if you have no children to worry about you, maybe you should worry about yourself, and just keep a bit in the pot, in case. These are judgements only you can make, and will depend on the care that's available, and what it costs, and the benefits and means tests that apply at the time. So, in essence, all this chapter is meant to do is point out that when we were younger, as Jenny Joseph's poem 'Warning' says, we had to 'pay the rent and not swear in the street'. That was when we did the careful, cautious thing. We worried about our responsibilities, and what people would think of us. That was the time in our lives when we thought spending on ourselves was as vulgar as food and vanity. Now things are different. Now I can, if I wish, as Jenny suggests, 'spend my pension on brandy and summer gloves, And satin sandals, and say we've no money for butter'. And if the world disapproves, let them.

Chapter Three

What Does 'Old' Look Like?

> *When I am an old woman I shall wear purple with a red hat which doesn't go . . .*

Jenny Joseph, 'Warning'

There was a time when old women wore black. 'Black bombazine' was the fashion, though I'm not sure what bombazine was. I have family pictures of my grandmothers and great-grandmothers dressed in black from head to foot. Partly that was because so many old ladies were widows and, like Queen Victoria, they remained in mourning for the rest of their lives. Partly it was because black was the uniform of the old. My grandmother Milly was a lively, humorous woman, and we loved each other dearly. One summer when she was in her late seventies she took me on holiday to a hotel in Eastbourne, but it wasn't to her taste. I remember her walking down one of the grand lounges waving her stick dismissively at the other residents as they sat dozing in their chairs. 'Look at all these old crocks!' she said. But vivacious as she was, Milly would never have worn purple with a red hat. Her shoes were sensible, her skirts well below the knee, and she wore black, or grey, or lilac, the discreet colours of the old lady.

Her underwear, too, belonged to a world long gone, and unlamented. Beneath her skirts Granny used to wear hefty silk bloomers with elasticated legs where, disconcertingly, she kept her handkerchief. She used to pull it out with a flourish, blow her nose gustily, and then return it to nestle around her knees until she needed it again. She also wore pink whalebone corsets completely encasing her bust, waist and hips. I used to watch her while she was dressing, pulling the strings tightly around her cottage-loaf shape. Even as a child, I was horrified to see her so ferociously imprison herself. She was the perfect cuddly granny but, my goodness, those corsets kept her firmly unliberated. She wore them because they were part of her uniform: she was dressing the part of an old woman.

Now my generation have become grandmothers, we dress very differently. Bloomers would be unthinkable. I have adopted the uniform of my daughters, jeans and thongs, and nobody looks askance. There is a streak of rebellion in my fashion sense: my clothes mean I'm thumbing my nose at the passing of time. I'm sure that's what Jenny Joseph meant with her purple and the red hat – she was expressing the rebellion of the over-fifties who don't want to be labelled 'elderly' or 'middle-aged', dull, modest and careful. So what if people call us mutton dressed as curly, girly lambs? We're too old now to be careful. The hell with what other people think of us, and our new-found confidence. The nonchalance of the new grannies is expressed in our dress. Grannies in Lycra, grannies in T-shirts, grannies in tropically brilliant colours are everywhere, blooming in the summer like dahlias. Pop into any high-street changing room and you may well find a granny alongside teenagers with pierced belly buttons. Not that I'd go quite as far as the aged swinger I once interviewed. Her name was Ivy and she was ninety, notorious in her seaside town for being the first on the disco dance floor and the last to leave it. Her mini-skirts sparkled with sequins, and after she had appeared on my talk show she propped up the bar for hours, knocking back the rum and Coke, while the researchers, all a quarter of her age, were longing to go home. Ivy had been a party-girl all her life and saw no reason to stop at ninety. Her energy was amazing, but she did present a slightly nightmarish vision of old age. Helen

Gurley Brown was also determined to beat the clock when I met her in her seventies at a smart publishing party. In the 1960s she had been the guru of the single girl, and founded *Cosmopolitan* with the iconic Cosmo girl. Almost single-handedly she had created a revolution for single women. She swept away the image of the sad spinster, the unmarried wallflower waiting on the shelf for a strong man to come along and give her life some meaning. Helen argued that women could be strong too, and glamorous and fun-loving, and great though marriage was, there were other ways to find fulfilment. Her best-selling titles, like *Sex and the Single Girl*, carried her message around the world. When I met her, her hair was immaculate, her makeup glossy, but her slender body (rigorously exercised each day) was tightly swathed in chiffon that stopped well above her knee, and her cleavage was almost entirely exposed. Clearly she was refusing to give in to time, and I applauded her attitude. But I wouldn't choose that path myself. Without surrendering, you can choose to take evasive action, rather than confronting age head on. There comes a time when courage becomes foolhardy, and I reckoned for Helen that time had come.

The sad truth is that nobody has yet invented a fountain of youth for us to bathe in. Those miracles don't yet happen. What we can do is pretend, and for creating illusion, and maintaining it, nobody could touch Marlene Dietrich. She was fabulous, and I suppose about seventy, when I saw her in concert, and her performance was engraved on my memory.

Maybe her curving wave of blonde hair was a wig. Perhaps it's true that her nude dress with a few discreetly placed spangles was hiding a tight pink rubber corset that held her upright. Certainly she was wearing heels so high they would have made a lesser mortal giddy, and she was trailing a white fox fur luxurious enough to drive any animal-rights lobbyist mad. From her daughter's biography, I gather that Marlene was often wheelchair-bound off-stage, but she could still stalk imperiously across the stage when she had to. And when I watched her she held the whole audience spellbound, whipping them into a standing ovation. They clearly believed she was infinitely sexy and completely ageless. She stopped performing when she was seventy-three, and from that moment, the legend goes, she took to her bed in her Paris flat, talking to her friends, many of whom were world leaders, around the world on the telephone. The last thing she wanted to do in her old age was shatter her own myth by being seen as she really was, wigless, in a wheelchair without a spangle or stiletto heel to camouflage her. But these days, when the paparazzi haunt every celebrity's doorstep with their long lenses, motivated by the knowledge that they can earn thousands of dollars worldwide with a single vindictive picture, Marlene would never get away with it.

There is one consolation for the voraciousness of today's cameras. If maintaining an illusion is impossible in real life, at least technology has brought Photoshop. This is the computer technique of manipulating an image, so that every unwanted line and wrinkle on a face can be erased; the computer can even thicken hair and lengthen a neck. I have seen Photoshopped pictures of myself I didn't recognise: my eyes were meltingly magnified, and my chin was tightened and softened, all without any of the pain or expense of surgery. I once wrote an article decrying this falsification, but I must admit that when I see that flattering Photoshopped picture used in a newspaper or a magazine I never ring up and complain. Honesty has its limits. The only trouble is, I dare not meet the magazine readers face to face. I know I can't possibly live up to that image in real life.

There are women who can: Twiggy, for instance. Lesley Hornby (Twiggy's real name before she became the face of the sixties) had the unfair advantage of perfect features – she was, after all, the world's most famous supermodel. Still a top model nearly fifty years later, it's not all that surprising that she has aged so beautifully, given her wide eyes, straight nose and long, slender proportions. (Not all famous beauties manage to grow old so triumphantly, though: think of Brigitte Bardot. But then, though the men who thrilled to her pouting lips, perfect French curves and tangled hair may now mourn her loss, to women there's something magnificent about Bardot's refusal to disguise the damage done by sun and gravity.) And now that Twiggy has been signed up by M & S, where she glides the rest of us can stumble in her path, for she is modelling clothes that are fashionable, flattering and, above all, affordable. That's the way to do it. No funereal bombazine for Twiggy, but no exposed cleavage or spangled mini-skirts either. Dame Helen Mirren also has lessons for us older women. Her style is as regal as that of the Queen she played so convincingly: the dress she wore to accept her Oscar was gold lace, revealing, but not exposing. On the world's biggest red-carpet stage she outshone women of half her age. Dame Helen proved that a woman can remain alluring even in her third age, because sex appeal happens in the mind.

But then again, that's not entirely true. In my mind I am for ever twenty-eight, which happened to be my favourite age. Some of my best middle-aged friends have decided to stick at seventeen. They refer to themselves as 'recycled teenagers'. Together we've taken the view that chronological age may creep inexorably on, but we will ignore mere numbers. It works, most of the time. Then, suddenly, we turn our heads as we pass a mirror and a stranger greets us. Who on earth is that grey-haired, wrinkled person who stares back at us, looking so alarmed? Oh, my God, it's me. The temptation, of course, is to look away quickly and walk on by. Sometimes I think we never evolved to cope with the destructive impact of the looking-glass. It's such a shock to watch yourself growing old, especially if you've ever been beautiful. That takes real courage. I remember the singer Eartha Kitt sitting in a BBC dressing room staring at herself in the mirror, an expression of terror on her face. I walked past, mystified. What had she got to be frightened of? She was the star Orson Welles had described twenty years earlier as the most exciting woman in the world. I thought she still looked fascinating, with her slanting eyes, her high cheekbones, her lips curling with mocking sensuality. I was in my thirties, and about to interview her. She was in her forties, and now I know what she was looking at in the mirror. With far less to lose, I now examine myself in the same way, I suspect many of us do, as we grow older. She was searching for the tiny lines around her eyes, the slight beginnings of a sag around her jaw, changes that were invisible to me but for her must have been like hearing a distant death knell.

It is intriguing that two of the greatest beauties of our time, Marilyn Monroe and Diana, Princess of Wales, both died at thirty-six. The film star and the princess were at their loveliest, at their most independent and at the height of their power; fans around the world worshipped them. Their faces on the cover of any magazine on earth were guaranteed to double its sales. They both devoted immense professional time and care to their appearance, knowing that their status depended upon it. Diana, in her Catherine Walker and Versace dresses, had created a personal style, classic but alluring. Monroe had herself sewn into clothes so tight she couldn't walk up steps without help, dresses held on by straps so fragile that they snapped at the perfect psychological moment in the middle of a press conference. We can still see them in our imagination, in full bloom. They never had time to wither or fade. Is it just chance that they both died on the cusp of middle age? Did the phantom of age, the inevitable crumbling of skin and sinew, haunt them, perhaps drive them to a tragically early death? Monroe, even if she didn't actually commit suicide, was notoriously careless with the prescription drugs she used to anaesthetise herself. Diana was killed in a car crash when a seat-belt could have saved her life, as it saved her bodyguard's. I can remember seeing pictures of her that last summer on jet skis, never wearing a life-jacket. A journalist reported seeing her fleeing from the paparazzi, driving herself recklessly into the thick of the traffic to get away from the pack that hounded her. Diana and Marilyn had both used their physical power like a calling card. They will never grow old now. Did they instinctively run away from their own future? Did they fear they would lose their power, that without beauty they would never be able to cope with age and ageing? Did they flirt with death, the only alternative?

Perhaps we're lucky that we haven't their extraordinary beauty, so we have much less to lose. In which case let's take a deep breath, steel ourselves, and stare back at the little old stranger in the mirror. It might be worth the pain. Because there are some easy, inexpensive sticking plasters to stick over the psychic wounds. Start by assessing your hair, if you still have any. Even if you haven't, baldness can be treated. A very famous male dancer friend was so concerned about the circle of pink skin on the top of his head that he painted it black. There are hair plugs, and transplants, and toupees, and for those who are never out in a high wind, the notorious comb-over. Thank goodness that fashion seems to have died out – the three long strands of hair stretched across a bald skull was never convincing. It was astonishing how many otherwise intelligent men adopted it. The modern solution is a number one, the shaved head that Yul Brynner, Telly 'Kojak' Savalas and Bruce Willis have made sexy. It gives a prize-fighter look, which suits some men, but not all.

Fortunately, baldness is not such a frequent problem for women. Not many women with alopecia have as lovely a face as Gail Porter, who displays her naked head as bravely as she once displayed her naked body in lights projected on to the Houses of Parliament in London. Most of us would prefer to hide a bald head or thinning hair under a wig, and wigs can be great fun. There is no need to spend hundreds of pounds on perfectly woven real hair, sold by Greek nuns. These days, there are shiny little nylon numbers in any colour, and many different styles, woven on to an elastic base, which stay attached and arranged even in a tempest, and cost a fraction of the real-hair versions. But then you have a dilemma: what colour do you want to be? With a wig you can be any colour you like, change with the weather, and the time of day. Without a wig, most women in time will naturally turn grey or white. Some of them look wonderful. The traditional English rose, with apple-blossom cheeks and sky-blue eyes, can look even more beautiful when their complexion is framed with a soft white halo. The striking Italian beauty, her raven hair streaked with white may also look dramatic. But most of us don't look better brindled like a feral cat. So the answer is, if you don't like it, dye it, and most people choose to become blonde. It has the softness of white, but it's a lot more fun, and don't worry if you find you have a completely new image. Dolly Parton once said, 'I'm not offended by all the dumb-blonde jokes because I know I'm not dumb . . . I also know I'm not blonde.' While we're on the subject of hair, the odd thing is that as time goes by you lose hair where you expect it to grow, but you find hair in the most unlikely places. Get rid of it. If it's new to you, and grows anywhere other than the scalp, less is more. I never understand why some men allow their eyebrows to beetle and their nostrils to bristle, especially when the solution is as close as the nearest pair of nail scissors. Women who suddenly grow new black moustaches are well advised to find a strong light, a magnifying mirror and a pair of square-ended tweezers. One famous and glamorous television presenter attended a charity event with her cheeks sprouting clumps of fine white hair like cotton-wool. It was a new look for her, but not a good one.

Having dealt with the hair, smile. There is a good reason behind this advice: a smile is the most effective beauty treatment. It gives the right context for laughter lines, it plumps up cheeks and it makes eyes sparkle. Even if you're feeling gloomy, smile and your mood will lift. But there's bad news, too. Sometimes when you smile you'll find it creates a little frown between your eyebrows, and lines across your forehead. Which means another decision. To Botox or not to Botox? Botox is not a solution to frowns and wrinkles, it's a stop-gap. An injection will only last three months or so, and then you'll need to renew it. It hurts, like a wasp sting, though that soon passes. And it must be administered by an expert who knows exactly where to place the needle to avoid blood vessels and bruising. There is also a very worrying rumour that Botox could migrate into the brain, and it certainly can lift your eyebrows so that they arch into a permanently infuriated expression. Another friend, a noted ageless beauty, recently arrived at my house for dinner looking furious. I had no idea what I had done to offend her, until I realised she had just had a Botox session with her cosmetic surgeon, and he had paralysed the muscles in her brow, sending her eyebrows skyward.

The only lasting solution to the passing of time is surgery – the face-lift, brow-lift and all the other little nips and tucks. Even they will sag in time, and need to be re-nipped after five years or so. But they will turn the clock back maybe ten years, provided you have the money to invest (several thousands of pounds) and the time, because you'll need to go into seclusion for at least three weeks to allow the bruising and swelling to subside.

If all that seems rather too drastic a solution to the stranger in the mirror, there are a million different anti-ageing cosmetics on the market that claim to 'diminish the appearance of fine lines'. Oh, yes? Maybe there is one that works, but if there is, I've never found it. The late, much-lamented Dame Anita Roddick got into terrible trouble with the rest of the cosmetics industry by saying that no cream or ointment will really make your skin look younger. She was telling the truth. All those unguents and treatments may make us feel better, and sometimes the more expensive they are, the better we feel. But that may also be the relaxing effect of having your face stroked, and some time to yourself. In which case the lesson must be, buy something cheap and basic, rather than some hugely luxurious cream filled with powdered llama hoof or whatever mystical ingredient is the one most in demand at the time. (For a television April Fool hoax I once invented an anti-wrinkle cream made out of rhinoceros spit. As far as I know, rhinoceroses don't spit. A month later a tabloid newspaper reported that a top pop star was using it. You see how credulous we are?)

So when the next film star tells us she has achieved her smooth brow and peach-like complexion just by drinking eight litres of spring water a day, you and I will know she's a liar. She's done it by spending time and money, and using a great deal of expert skill. Is it possible for the rest of us, if we work really hard, to look as glamorous as Joan Collins at seventy? Sadly, no, because to look like Joan Collins now, we would have had to look like Joan Collins then, and I have it on good authority (from Larry Hagman, who squired her when she was a Rank starlet and told me so) that she was by far the most beautiful young actress of her generation, and they included Elizabeth Taylor. Mind you, even Joan works out, and has professional skill with makeup and fashion; she also has a handsome young husband, and keeps her face out of the sun, even in St Tropez. Best of all, she's very funny, and there's no doubt that laughter is the fountain of youth, and the best aphrodisiac. What's more, she uses Vaseline on her face.

So what does 'old' look like? It should look as if you are comfortable in your skin. It may have been tightened by dozens of face-lifts, if that's what you want, or it may have delicate wrinkles all over it like an autumn leaf, because that can be beautiful too. Your clothes may be sophisticated and elegant, or mischievous as a teenager's. The important thing is that when you look at that stranger in the mirror, you smile at each other. Diana and Marilyn got it wrong. Eartha need not have been terrified. Marlene should not have taken to her bed. Growing older is not a penance, or a punishment, it's a reward. It should be fun, and it helps if you look as if you're having fun, because that way you don't just convince other people, you convince yourself. So on with the purple and the red hat – or, better still, the red wig – and enjoy!

Chapter Four

Loss

> "*Grief is the price we pay for love*"

Her Majesty the Queen

So much about getting older is the familiar see-saw between good news and bad . . . wrinkles collect under our eyes, but our ever-more bleary eyesight means we are spared too clear a reflection. We can't for the life of us remember what we did last week, but memories of forty years ago are as sharp as ever. Our reflexes may not be fast enough for us to win at snap, but we are crafty enough to beat the crowd at poker. So the reassuring truth about growing older is that, in many ways, whatever time takes from us, it gives back more, and we gain at least as much as we lose. However, and this is a big however, there is one aspect of ageing that has no redeeming feature. No matter how optimistic and positive we are, or try to be, one truth we cannot avoid: passing time brings with it the loss of those we love and care about. Inevitably, as we grow older, we outlive some of those closest to us. And, of course, the longer we survive, the more friends, family, lovers and colleagues we lose.

Grief is the price we pay for love. The Queen is not renowned for making memorable speeches (perhaps that is one of the secrets of her success), but when she used that brief, eloquent phrase (in the service held in New York on the anniversary of the Twin Towers tragedy) the congregation sighed with recognition. Everything has its price, and love, the greatest gift of all, carries the greatest price. In my experience, bereavement is an experience most of us never fully recover from. Part of the shock is because we have become so unfamiliar with death. These days we try hard to protect ourselves from that one great inevitability. It was not always so. When illnesses were mysterious, and germs were unknown, each new plague and epidemic brought coffins out into the street. It was common for them to be open, so that mourners could pay their respects face to face. Popular entertainment often included touching death scenes. But with modern medicine, and hospitals built and run like huge factories, we have become hermetically sealed against the reality of death. The myth has grown up that we can conquer illness, even turn back the clock and stay for ever young. We have disinfected our modern, civilised world to be free from unpleasantness, like death or decay, and tried to pretend we're immortal. And all through my childhood, the pretence worked. But when I was in my late teens a lovely young woman, extremely intelligent but chronically depressed, killed herself. Her brother was one of my closest friends. I remember sitting with him, and hearing him blame himself for not having been able to save her. I tried, in vain, to assure him that hers was the most personal decision of all, and that he must not feel in any way responsible. It was a crucial lesson for me. Suicide creates many victims, and a ripple of suffering spreads outwards through family and friends.

When I went to university, and joined a student company who performed at the Edinburgh Festival, one of the other performers was an attractive, talented girl called Liz. We became great friends, and I went to her home for lunch. I noticed that while the rest of us were eating a simple snack, her mother had cooked her fillet steak. When Liz was out of the room for a moment, I said to her mother, 'Be careful with Liz. It's exhausting, doing a student tour like ours.' I still remember her mother's face. I didn't know that Liz had leukaemia, for which, then, there was no cure. Liz's mother had made the conscious decision to allow her to spend as much time as possible enjoying the fun of our student company, rather than spending the last few months with her. It was an extraordinary sacrifice, and when I understood it, I was enormously impressed. When Liz died, I had two lasting memories. One was of the waste of that charming, talented young woman. The other was of the grief, dignity and sacrifice of her mother. Again I learned a valuable lesson. The death of a child leaves a scar that never heals. And yet, although the death of a child is something no parent can get over, there may be ways of moving past, of surviving what feels at the time to be a total barrier to hope and happiness. In my forties, when I was working on *That's Life!*, we started a campaign to save the life of a toddler, Ben Hardwick. Ben, then aged two, suffered from biliary atresia, a serious liver disease. His mother Debbie rang our programme in desperation to tell us that Ben's illness would kill him in a matter of days if he didn't receive a liver transplant. In those days transplants had almost entirely stopped, because of public trepidation that organs might be removed from patients before they were dead. Ben's surgeon, Professor Sir Roy Calne, told Debbie that to save Ben's life would require a total change in public opinion. At twenty-two she was unfazed: nothing is impossible when you are fighting for your baby's life. 'How can I change it?' she asked.

'Television is the most powerful medium,' Sir Roy told her.

Television had never been used in that way before. Certainly on *That's Life!* we were accustomed to trying to achieve justice for consumers, but not to saving life. I think if we had asked permission from the bosses, they would have decided this was way beyond our brief. But we didn't ask permission, and fortunately Debbie neither knew nor cared about the etiquette of programme-making. She lived in West London, where many television professionals lived and worked. They gave her our number and she rang *That's Life!*. I still remember the excitement of the young researcher who found me in the dreary BBC canteen at lunchtime to tell me Ben's story, and that he had only a few days to live. Suddenly I stopped comparing congealed baked beans with slushy garden peas, and sent him away to find a director and a film crew to film Ben that afternoon. As an afterthought I said, 'Buy some of that bubble mixture you get from toy shops.' My son Joshua, almost exactly the same age as Ben, loved watching bubbles float around him, trying to catch them before they popped and disappeared.

The film arrived the next day in our cutting room, and I remember Ben's face as he sat in his bath watching the bubbles float around him. He was a gorgeous child: his huge blue eyes were fringed with heavy dark lashes and his smile melted your heart. It certainly melted the hearts of millions of viewers who heard Debbie pleading with the eloquence born of desperation. One week later a donor was found. The wife of a consultant anaesthetist working in Nottingham had seen our programme, and told her husband. One of his patients, a fragile little boy called Matthew Fewkes, tragically died that week, and the doctor asked the family whether they would consent to his liver being used to save Ben's life. They agreed. So, thanks to the Fewkeses' generosity and compassion, the operation took place. By then the story had seized the nation's imagination. Eighteen million viewers watched, week by week, as it unfolded. As a direct consequence, not just Ben but many other children also had the life-saving operations they desperately needed. Transplant surgery was back on the agenda and hundreds of lives were saved. Tragically, Ben only lived another year. I heard the news of his death in the early hours of the morning, woken by a phone call from a local journalist. The production team who had grown so close to Debbie were stunned, but we had no time to grieve. We put together a film celebrating Ben's short life, and made plans for a memorial fund in his name. The Ben Hardwick Memorial Fund paid for an intensive-care bed for children in Addenbrooke's Hospital, and I learned another lesson.

Of course, not everyone has access to a televised campaign that turns a child into a national hero. But I have met many parents who have raised money in their child's memory, even started charities and support groups to help other families in the same situation. From their extraordinary achievements I have learned that it is possible to transmute grief into something strong and positive, even when you are suffering from the agonising impact of a beloved child's death, if you can create a lasting memorial. Debbie Hardwick knows that to this day her son is remembered, and that his example has saved countless lives.

Deaths are as different, as individual, as births. Two of the deaths that had an impact on my life were less like the brutal chopping of a sweet young sapling, more the quiet fall of a grand old tree. My own parents died, my father Harry at ninety, my mother Katherine at ninety-three. I miss them still, but I don't feel cheated. I have the consolation that they had both lived full, rich lives. Not that they were famous or flamboyant: they spent most of their lives in the privet-lined streets of Cricklewood in north-west London. They enjoyed family parties and occasional holidays, going to the local cinema and taking coffee in the shopping mall. My father was an opera buff; my mother was a governor of a children's day nursery until almost the end of her life. They both loved bridge and Scrabble, squabbling amicably about their wilder attempts to win. If that sounds dull or uneventful, then perhaps it was, measured by the standards of tabloid headlines. But their lives were also filled with laughter, and curiosity, and nurturing relationships. Of course, they also had had their difficulties and frustrations, as we all have. But they lived caring, careful lives, and their deaths were, in a sense, a celebration of that achievement. My husband Desmond Wilcox's death was different. It was in no way part of my life's plan that my partner, best friend and soul-mate should die at sixty-nine. Not that I have ever planned anything in my life. I always think that trying to predict and decide in advance means cutting oneself off from exciting, unanticipated adventures. But Desi and I had definitely decided that when he retired we would explore Britain together, going to all the nooks and crannies of this delicious island he knew, and I didn't. But it was not to be. Of course I knew he had heart disease – he'd had his first by-pass fifteen years earlier, then made brief but sincere attempts to give up his life-long addiction to pâté and pork pies. He tried, even more briefly, to survive on a 'healthy heart' diet of beans and lentils, although the social consequences were pretty drastic. But soon things returned to normal, and we both decided that it was the quality of life that mattered, rather than the quantity. Even so, I feel cheated. And here, too, I learned a tough lesson. Don't put off your dreams, especially if there is someone to share them with. There is no guarantee that tomorrow will arrive for you, or for you both. *Carpe diem.*

Tomorrow arrived harshly for me, in September 2000, and I was unprepared for it. They warn you about a great many things when you get married. Consult any agony column and you'll find yards of advice about how, and if, to stay faithful, what to do if he won't help with the washing-up, and how to cope if he insists on trying on your suspender belt. But nobody gives you any advice at all about the most difficult, painful problem of all. How to carry on with your life if the husband you loved and shared it with dies before you. How to walk the lonely path from wife to widow. It's a lesson many of us women have to learn the hard way. Men are, after all, the frailer sex. Forget their machismo, their muscles, all that hunter-gathering: men lack the physical stamina for living, so women last on average ten years longer. That's if you're on a level playing-field. But if, like me and many other women, you are attracted to talented, experienced older men, their extra years make your widowhood even more likely.

I was reminded of this when I attended the funeral of Alan Coren, writer, humorist, wit and national treasure. Among all his many, many friends and admirers on that cold, grey autumn day when, physically and spiritually, the clouds had rolled over to obscure the sunlight, there was a group of us widows whose eyes were on Anne Coren, the beautiful, clever wife he adored, and left behind. She was immensely courageous in her grief, staying calm and elegant, and managing to comfort all her family and friends, but we knew, we widows, what she would be facing in the days and weeks ahead.

Not that there is an established map, or a rule-book you can follow in bereavement, but that doesn't inhibit people from trying to impose their ideas on you. That's one of the first things you discover as a widow. People around you, with your best interests at heart, shower you with instructions. You must cry more. Or cry less. Go out more. Or stay at home and grieve. Go to counselling. Move house. Stay where you are. Wear black. Wear scarlet. You get more advice from caring friends when you're numb and vulnerable with grief than you ever get when you face other life milestones, like being pregnant or trying to deal with toddlers' and teenagers' tantrums. So, the first piece of advice I would give any new widow is ignore all the advice and do what your own heart tells you to do.

It is said that the English vice is reticence, and that we won't talk to the bereaved about their loss for fear of hurting them. But as a widow myself, aged sixty when Desmond died, I found myself surrounded by people who put their heads caringly on one side when we met, and asked, in tones of husky compassion, 'How *are* you?' I never knew how to answer. Should I bravely smile and say, 'Fine!' or would that be perceived as uncaring? Should I let my face crumple and just sigh, or would that be construed as surrendering to grief? In the end I used to say, 'Ah, well, you know . . .' and let them finish the sentence themselves. On the other hand, while we widows are dealing with our own pain as best we can, it is important that someone considers the children and how they are coping. I have met bereaved children who have been locked into silence by their friends and families who thought, wrongly, that by ignoring their pain they could make it go away. My own children were almost adult when their father died, but even so, looking back, I feel guilty that in dealing with my own grief I neglected theirs. Particularly my son Joshua's: he instantly took on his father's role of protecting me when Desi died, but at great cost to himself. He had to find ways later of dealing with his loss, and now I believe I could have helped more effectively and sooner.

Recently I went to the first great hospice in this country, St Christopher's, in South London, founded by Dame Cicely Saunders, to attend their Candle group specially created to support bereaved young people. It was a moving and inspiring evening. In the safety of a room filled with other young people who completely understood, each one was emboldened to talk about the father, mother or sibling they had lost. There are now charities that provide help for bereaved children, like Winston's Wish, showing them, for instance, how to create a memory box as a source of comfort and a memorial. This is one way a widow's friends and family can offer valuable constructive help, to keep an eye open for children and young people who may be relegated to the next room, and are feeling left out, or guilty, or bewildered by the changes in their lives, and the uproar of feeling they are experiencing.

There are so many changes to bewilder us, when death comes and rips the heart out of our lives. The newly empty bed feels like a desert. The first Christmas is a horrendous hurdle. That was another mistake I made, trying faithfully to re-create all the things we used to do when Desmond was alive, even to the same carol concert for friends and neighbours in our cottage. My daughters retreated in tears: the familiar music just made the emptiness of his chair more agonising. Now we deliberately do everything differently, so as not to exacerbate our pain, but that was a lesson I had to learn.

Friendships, in my experience, dwindle in number, but the few that remain deepen. There is no doubt that I get fewer invitations now, seven years after Desi's death, than we did as a couple. That's understandable. I was married to a man who, like Alan Coren, brought light and laughter into the room with him. Without him I, as a single (and, as perhaps my female ex-friends suspected, possibly predatory) female, am a liability at a dinner party. They really needn't worry about my motives. I'm not going to snuggle up to their husbands for warmth. I have learned over the past seven years that the only thing worse than losing your soul-mate is to be chased around the kitchen by someone you don't fancy, who doesn't make you laugh and whom you could never love. There may be widows whose hair, as Oscar Wilde said, turns bright gold with shock, and who go out on the prowl. But few of the widows I know have found a replacement in their hearts or in their homes for the love they lost.

Not that it wouldn't be helpful, sometimes, in practical terms to find a new man. There are lightbulbs I can't reach. Bills and bank statements are a frightening incomprehensible tangle if, like me, you used to leave them to your capable husband. Mine was a foreign correspondent before he became a documentary-maker, so he adored travel and was very good at it. I, on the other hand, have been known to confuse east with west in moments of stress. So planning holidays was a skill I had to learn and, like many widows, I have become addicted to cruising, which removes most of the strain. There was the horrible experience of calling in the wrong plumber, who created havoc in the house and left blocked loos and leaking pipes behind him. I know Desi would have spotted his incompetence far sooner, and got rid of him before he could do all that expensive damage. And all this new technology creates a jungle of new decisions: how soon should I buy an iPhone, do I throw out all the clumsy old-fashioned televisions, when should I change the car? Some women like and understand machinery. I don't and can't.

The men I've spoken to who have been left alone after divorce or bereavement are often just as heartbroken and bewildered. Many widowers feel that without their wife or partner they have lost the whole point of their existence. Even if it happens comparatively late in life, age does not mean you hurt less, nor that you can make cool decisions. The memory of all the years you shared is a spiritual home to you, now you find yourself in exile. It will take time to come to terms with the new world surrounding you. Some widowers rage against their loss, turn their backs on their well-meaning friends and family, draw their curtains and lock their doors. They feel safer alone. Withdrawal is a self-protective reflex, but the truth is that in the end it may harm more than it heals; the medicine may turn to poison. Take your time, and when you are ready to venture out you may well find that it is easier than you feared, and more enjoyable. A single man with a smile is welcome anywhere, socially, professionally, or as a volunteer in a good cause. In some cases what begins with a work relationship or a friendship can end in partnership or even marriage. Even if it doesn't, you may return home from a day spent with a new team, or a set of friends, with a real sense of achievement, and of a day well spent.

The danger, it seems to me, is when a vulnerable partner, man or woman, seeks consolation by trying to replace exactly what they have lost. Then, like Paul McCartney, they can be driven by loneliness to let hope triumph over judgement, and allow themselves to be misled. Heather Mills was not Linda, and could never be, as Paul found out to his cost. (I watched their story unfold when I worked with Heather, as I will explain later.) Yet who can blame him? There is no more vulnerable word than 'alone', even if you are the richest, most famous, most adored musician in the world. The fact is that even without a partner to share your life, you are still you. Above all, the advice I would give any new widow or widower, and I really will try to restrain myself, is, don't imagine your life has ended too, though it may feel that way at first. You will find a new path. You will not be alone, unless you want to be. There are people who will clamour for your skills, your company, your friendship and your love. Though your partner may have left your life, the soul-mate you have lost is still there, in your heart, loving and cheering you on. So for their sake, embrace and enjoy your new life. It's what they would most have wanted.

Chapter Five

Moving On

> *You can live to be a hundred if you give up all the things that make you want to be a hundred*

Woody Allen

mong the many skills I don't have but envy, like tap-dancing and car maintenance, is moving on. I stayed in the same job for thirty years, and in the same relationship for more than thirty years. I've lived in the same city for nearly sixty years. As my friends and colleagues change jobs and homes and partners, I watch them with the kind of envy a scarecrow probably feels when he sees ramblers wandering past. There's no doubt I'm a stick-in-the-mud. And yet I know that moving on is important because I heard the Queen say so. (Well, there are other reasons, but that one will do to kick off the chapter.) We were together in Buckingham Palace with, I suppose, five hundred other guests at a special reception she held for 'people of sixty plus who are still making a difference'. When I received the invitation I was thrilled, and I admit the very large gold-rimmed card stayed on my mantelpiece long after the party had come and gone. The reception was splendid but, then, it had certain advantages. For one thing, a palace is a terrific venue for a party – all that space, acres of red carpet and gold-rimmed ceilings. It's a theatrical setting, and someone once told me that at the end of one 'do' in Buckingham Palace he witnessed the senior staff, who are no doubt ex-sea lords or something equally elevated, leave through a door concealed in the panelling and suddenly change into ordinary middle-aged men in a comparatively shabby corridor, hanging up their frills and furbelows and swapping notes, just like the cast of a matinée of *Cinderella*: 'I thought that went well, didn't you?' 'Yes, the guests were happy, apart from the two ugly old girls with big feet' . . . and so on. The other advantage Buckingham Palace has is the hostess. She is littler than you might imagine, but when the Queen walks through her guests she creates a kind of wave, a wave of people moving first away, as they register her approach and shift nervously on to the back foot, then forward again, as they join the crowd, petrified they might not be introduced. I remember one very senior charity executive going bright red in the face with fury at the thought of missing out on a royal handshake. Which is understandable, but even if he had, the other guests are usually so interesting they keep one amused.

At this reception for the over-sixties I had the entertaining experience of meeting David Hockney, who is not only one of our greatest artists but a rampant and militant smoker, who demands equal rights with non-smokers, and said so with wit and style. As the Queen approached from the other end of the room, I looked around and spotted Sir Nicholas Winton, one of my heroes. He rescued a generation of Czech Jewish children by putting them on trains from Prague just as the Nazis were invading, and found families to look after them in Britain. For years his achievement had been forgotten, not least by him, and the children themselves had no idea who had been responsible for saving them from the Holocaust. I was very fortunate that my programme *That's Life!* was responsible for discovering the story and reuniting 'the British Schindler', as he has been called, with the children (now adults, of course) he had saved. From then on many of them called themselves 'Winton's Children', which we took as the title of the documentary we made about him. Since then Nicky has not only received a knighthood, but was nominated for a Nobel Peace Prize. When I saw him at the reception he was sitting quietly with his son on gilt chairs at the side of one of the great rooms. I went over to them just as the Queen arrived. I couldn't resist the opportunity of introducing them to her. 'Your Majesty,' I said, 'may I present Sir Nicholas Winton?' and I gave her a brief summary of his achievements. 'What's more,' I finished, 'after the war, he put the children's pictures and documents into a briefcase, and forgot about it for forty years, until one day he and his wife were going through some stuff they had in their loft, and she found the case. He hadn't told her anything about it.'

'Quite right,' said the Queen. 'Move on. It's much the best thing.'

Well, Sir Nicholas may be able to, and the Queen may approve of it, but I find I get hopelessly stuck. I wonder whether many of us suffer from an inescapable nostalgia for times and places, people and pets, clothes and music, things that meant so much to us in our youth, and we cling to in our middle years. I spent a happy suburban childhood in North-west London and, like an elderly homing pigeon, I have returned there. My favourite countryside holidays as a child were in the New Forest in Hampshire, and now I have a cottage a few hundred yards away from my cousin's house in Bramshaw village where I spent so many happy days. My family and friends were noisy, argumentative and loving, and those are still the kind of people I feel most at home with.

'Mirror, mirror on the wall, I am my mother after all,' says the sign in my hallway.

Some people are admirably efficient when it comes to cutting themselves adrift from their past if it threatens to clog them or weigh them down. I have come across people who are chameleons, and manage to adapt themselves completely to a brand-new background. They are quite unsentimental, and make the most extraordinary changes in their lives and in themselves. One girl, I'll call her Lucy, I first met when we were both quite young. She looked startlingly like Brigitte Bardot then, overflowing with young, luscious sex appeal, but she sounded more like Eliza Doolittle pre-Professor Higgins, with her mouth full of South London glottal stops. In her late teens Lucy met a rich young man, and he introduced her to the extraordinary world of trust-fund heirs and heiresses. These were the young people who jetted around the world, gambled and overdosed on every possible sensation. They took the view that money was the passport to everything and everywhere. Lucy told me at the time that one of her wealthiest friends was a university student who never attended a class or a lecture, or deigned to write an essay. Instead, he hired his tutor to have dinner with him once a week, obviously believing he could take in all the knowledge he needed like a bowl of soup, painlessly. He failed his finals.

The impact of these gilded young people had a very odd effect on Lucy's language. Instead of her original Cockney

57

roughness, which was at least genuine, she started to attempt the clipped, high-pitched, strangulated vowels of the English upper classes. The result was that she was as screechy and unmusical as the most untalented parrot. But upper-classness was only a passing stage in her life. Her vitality and beauty were very soon picked up by Youth Television, who asked her to present one of the trendiest shows of the time. She dropped her upper-class vowels overnight, and went back to the Cockney she had grown up with, which had far more street-cred. That, too, was replaced when she went to the USA, first as part of the pop-music industry, latterly as an artist in California. When we last met, I was enchanted to find her in her third age, dressed in flowing draperies, with a soft American drawl in her voice, and a predilection for incense and crystals. While she was reading my astrological chart, I didn't dare mention to her the infinite number of Lucys I have known, because with each new persona she seemed to create a whole new outlook, and had cut the umbilical cord. She had absolutely no connection with her own past. I envied the number of lives she had lived, the many new faces, new voices, and totally different lifestyles she had adopted. Perhaps as the years go by we should all follow her example, and try to find new, but no less interesting, images for ourselves.

It will require self-discipline. For instance, moving on will mean turning our backs on ourselves as we once were. Lucy no longer dresses in plunging pink gingham, as she did in her Bardot phase. Following her lead, I have just thrown away my fishnet stockings. 'Move on,' I told myself sternly. 'You may still mentally be twenty-eight, but physically the legs have done considerably more mileage.' It was a struggle, coming to terms with that truth, and I wondered why. Perhaps the reason we older women are fatally attracted to fishnet stockings is because in our youth they used to be regarded as exotic, and slightly wicked. Parisian ladies of the night wore them posing under street-lamps, wearing tight black skirts and spiky stilettos. Fishnets are supposed to flatter legs of any shape and size, skinny or pudgy, so even the baggiest knees can be disguised by a latticework of black elastic. Above all, like those other fashion atrocities, dark red finger nails and gold ankle chains, fishnets were supposed to be irresistibly sexy. It's difficult to face the fact that you are no longer alluring. Even your ovaries retired long ago.

But I have had to move on and face the fact that the sexiness was pretty trashy and only the young can get away with that. Marilyn Monroe playing a saloon singer in *Bus Stop* famously found some fishnet tights in the 20th Century Fox wardrobe, and tore a hole in them so that she could sing 'That Old Black Magic' with the right kind of slutty intensity. When I was in my twenties I met Desmond, my future husband, in the BBC Club and he always said he was drawn to the sight of my fishnet stockings with a tear in them just above the knee. Not that I modelled myself on Marilyn, just that I'd got dressed in a hurry that morning. Desi and I got married ten years later, so something must have worked. But what may be OK when you're twenty, or even thirty, should be carefully reconsidered when you're over fifty. They may be fun on the young, but on the mature lady, fishnets look like a frantic attempt to turn back the clock.

I'm not advocating jettisoning everything we've enjoyed wearing, or lifestyles that have always suited us, just pointing out that it may be a symptom of a mind-set that has outlived its sell-by date. My generation is particularly vulnerable to getting stuck, metaphorically, in fishnets because we can remember the time when they were fashionable, and we needed them. In the eighties, when we first went into power dressing, with wide padded shoulders and heavy gold earrings, the message was clear: we are as tough as men are; we can push our way to the best jobs and the highest salaries. But underneath the uniform we wore Wonderbras, suspender belts and black stockings to seduce intimidated men. 'Don't be scared,' was the underlying message. 'We women are still feminine. We may be tigers in the boardroom, but we'll purr when we're patted.' The ferocious parliamentarian Edwina Currie was notorious for her sharp red jackets and her black stockings. The Prime Minister, John Major, couldn't resist them. But that was then. Now that ecology and fitness have overtaken con-spicuous expenditure, we women are keeping mind and body up to date by pounding along in trainers down at the gym every morning alongside the men, and pretty foolish we'd look doing that in criss-cross stockings.

I realised my own error not long ago, when I was well into my sixties, and my picture appeared in a popular magazine, my legs shamelessly encased in fishnet tights. Here's my excuse, m'lud. When *Closer* magazine invited me into a photographic studio by suggesting that I pose for a fashion shoot for the more mature woman, I visualised a smart little Chanel suit. When I arrived, all they had on the rail was a wisp of chiffon and a pair of fishnets. Of course I could have refused, and walked out. But then a thought struck me: how often in the future would anyone ask me to pose in such stuff? Next time they might bring out the granny shawl and carpet slippers. This might be my last chance to be a floozy. So, not only did I put on the fishnets and chiffon, I even threw caution to the wind and my legs into the air. My daughters screamed and laughed when they saw the picture; my son has still not forgiven me.

It taught me a lesson. The very odd fan-mail I received as a result showed me that fishnet stockings, like red suspenders, bring out a distressing masochism in British men. Never having seen myself as Miss Whiplash, handcuffs not being my thing, I resented the effect my *Closer* encounter had created. So I told myself it was time to move on. When you're over fifty, bite the bullet and give up leather skirts and navel-plunging cleavages. Not because we've lost our sex appeal, but because softness and sweetness go better with maturity than looking like a tough old boot. Being too 'up for it' smacks of desperation, and we don't want that, do we?

The second major decision in my recent life, far more difficult than chucking out my fishnets, was to recognise that I could no longer be a pet owner. Many older people can, and for them it's a scandal that a huge number of retirement flats and bungalows forbid them to take their dogs, cats and canaries with them. Dogs are good for you. They force you to take exercise. Stroking a cat lowers your blood pressure. What's more, when you walk around your home talking to yourself, you can always pretend you're talking to the canary. But I no longer have a partner, or children at home, to give continuity to my life. Every now and again I have to up sticks and travel, or spend the day wandering the country lecturing, and that would mean leaving a pet alone, which would be quite wrong. Once again, this was borne in on me because of a mistake I nearly made.

I'd given a birthday party in my garden, the rain held off, and the pink champagne held out. At sunset one guest left to re-park his car, and came back grey-faced. 'There's a large Alsation dog attacking your dustbins,' he said. 'It's barking ferociously at anyone who tries to get into your drive.' I went to the front door and saw the dog slinking past like a ghost. It was gaunt and grey in the twilight. I shouted angrily at it, and it fled.

The next morning I had an early meeting, but when I opened my front door to leave, I saw the dog lying on the step. Its great head was on my doormat, its long bony legs were crossed, it looked completely lifeless. I felt horrified, and guilty. It had obviously crawled back to my door to die. As I watched, I saw its chest move just a little. Maybe it wasn't completely dead. A vets' clinic had just opened at the end of my road, so just before I left I rang them and explained. 'It's dead, or almost,' I said. 'Can you collect it?' And then I added, knowing I was being daft, rash and sentimental, 'If you can save the dog, I'll keep it.'

My meeting took most of the day, but when I switched my mobile phone on again, there was a message.

'You've got a lovely dog.'

I rang the vet at once.

She said, 'We've rehydrated him, and he's quite lively now.'

'Ferocious?'

'Not at all. Very friendly.'

'I'll come and collect him.'

On my way home I tried to analyse why I wanted this dog. It was completely irrational. I've never much liked macho dogs like German Shepherds. The only reason even to consider taking this new stranger into my life was that I had the feeling maybe someone, somewhere, had brought him to my door on purpose.

I am not superstitious. I don't believe in spirits trying to get in touch, or voices from the grave. But Desmond was a terrific organiser. Though I hardly dared admit it, I couldn't help wondering. Had Desi organised this dog for me, as a birthday present? The timing was perfect. The dog arrived in my life not simply on the very day of my party, but that weekend my three children announced that they were considering leaving home. I was brave about it, they were all over twenty-five, and I smiled brightly whenever they talked about finding flats and flatmates. But if they did leave I knew it was going to be a very different life for me, rattling around our achingly empty family home. Desi, I knew, would worry for me. Two years before, Arthur, our beloved black Labrador had died. I hadn't been able to replace him, and he had been such a comforting presence in my life. At moments of grief, Arthur would put his head on my knee, or lie like a huge beanbag on my feet. He was also my unofficial personal trainer, forcing me to walk three times a day, every day, whatever the weather. Since I'd lost Arthur, I had become markedly lazier and less fit. Maybe Desi was worried about that, too. So after my meeting I went to the vet to collect the odd birthday present Destiny or Desi had sent me. I took my son Joshua with me, home from university, a great dog-lover. The vet brought the German Shepherd to us on a lead. Peter (his name came to me instantly, something to do with Peter Pan trying to come home to his mother) came straight up to us, wagging his tail. 'Sit,' I said. Peter sat instantly, and offered me his right paw. Someone had once cared enough about this dog to train him. Why, then, was he so painfully thin? Stroking him I could feel every rib, each vertebra. His long back sloped downwards, and there wasn't a shred of muscle left on his back legs to hold them straight. How long had he been abandoned to starve? How many weeks had he roamed the streets before he found my dustbins, and crept on to my doormat to die? The vet warned me that Peter's stomach might well be in uproar, if he'd been scavenging for weeks. While she talked to me, Peter looked into my eyes, with a deep, focused gaze. In my experience dogs only do that when they have something important to say. Peter's message was clear. Take me home. Joshua walked him back to our house and they played together in the garden. At one point Peter stood up on his frail back legs and put his paws on Joshua's shoulders. They were the same height. This was a very large dog indeed.

The next day I was filming in the country when I had a frantic phone call from my daughter Becca. 'How could you bring a dog into the house when you know nothing about it? It's ill and I've had to clear up a horrible mess all over the house.' I rushed home. We rang the local council, and they sent round a dog warden, Terry, a charming man. Not the frightening figure I'd imagined at all, no rifle or net. He explained that he takes stray dogs to Battersea Dogs and Cats Home, and they rehabilitate and rehome them. I couldn't bear the thought of abandoning Peter, but Terry said all I had to do was register an interest in him and I would have first refusal.

For the next few weeks I ricocheted between anxiety and

relief. Battersea, a great institution that sums up more about Britain than any public monument, is staffed by an army of dog-lovers. They are passionate, devoted and skilled. Would that we treated our unwanted children as compassionately and well as Battersea treats our stray dogs. They bathed him, X-rayed his hips, gave him antibiotics, vaccinated and micro-chipped him. His fur fluffed out, his digestion improved, and he began to put on weight. I visited him regularly. Then, on a Sunday about five weeks after he'd found me, I went down with a rug in the boot of my car, ready to take Peter home again.

When I arrived, the experts at Battersea told me there was one more hurdle for Peter to cross. Pat, their animal behaviourist, had to gauge his temperament, to make sure he was safe. He wasn't. When they introduced him to other dogs Peter revealed he was the Frank Sinatra of German Shepherds. Male dogs were there to fight, bitches were for his pleasure. Pat advised that if I took him for walks where there were many other dogs around I might well have to muzzle him and keep him on a lead.

I hated that idea. As I led Peter back to his kennel or, rather, if I'm to be honest, a newly strong, eager German Shepherd tugged me through the corridors, I realised that, like many other vulnerable older ladies, I had fallen for a young male who would cause chaos in my life. Suppose he ate my neighbour's dog? Or bonked all the local bitches? Suppose he attacked the window-cleaner or the postman? As the Battersea staff patiently told me, 'You don't want him to become a dog with a bad history. He needs to live somewhere semi-rural, to be owned by an enthusiast who will take him to a training school and instil some kind of discipline in him.'

There's no question that he stole a part of my heart when he crawled on to my doorstep, too weak to move. Ten years earlier, when I had a far more static life, and many more support systems, I would have kept him. As it was, I recognised my life had radically changed, and I must adjust my own horizons. So I told Battersea, sadly but realistically, that they should find another, more suitable home for him. With typical efficiency they did: he's living in the countryside with a lady who already owns a German Shepherd, so Peter will have company and a kindly, experienced owner. They've sent me a picture, and he's glowing with health and happiness. Something in me is deeply relieved.

My greatest area of failure to move on is a total inability to move house. Some years ago my accountant did a complex sum proving that our cottage in the New Forest, which I had managed to visit six times in twelve months, was costing me thirty thousand pounds of taxed income a year. Even I with my O-level maths could do that sum. Five thousand pounds a visit. Of course, if I spent longer in the cottage the cost would come down, but every time the sun shone and the road to Hampshire looked inviting, I found myself making excuses to stay in London. The reason we had made time to go to the cottage was the love and care Desi had lavished on it. Every quarry tile, each window latch was carefully and lovingly chosen. In the early-morning sunshine we used to walk together round the rose-beds, orange juice in hand, soaking up the delights of grasses and lilies tumbled together. Just before we left each Sunday night, he and I would run round the garden again, imprinting it on our memories as an investment for the week ahead. It was incredibly precious to both of us, but without him my loneliness intensified and I saw his ghost everywhere. No wonder I'd only stayed at the cottage six weekends, but at five thousand pounds a visit, the cost seemed wildly spendthrift. Could I bring myself to rent it out, to cover the expense? It would be a wrench for all of us to give it up – my father has a copper beech planted in his memory next to one of the tiny ponds, Desi's ashes are sprinkled on the hill behind the house, some of my children's happiest summers were spent playing on the lawn. All the same, half-heartedly, but knowing it was the rational thing to do, I asked an estate agent to call round and inspect it.

Suddenly things began to happen far faster than I had hoped. An ex-army family arrived, desperate to find a place to rent. One of their children had a place in a local school, but they had nowhere to stay. They walked around the cottage and garden, then came back to the kitchen and the wife told me, 'We've fallen in love.'

Well, that was difficult to resist. I went through the

agonies of de-cluttering, shredding thousands (literally) of letters, giving much-loved baggy sweaters to Oxfam, and sending obsolete machinery to the dump. I made a date with a local removal and storage firm, and booked it for Monday. On the Friday before they were due, the estate agent rang. At the very last moment the family had pulled out, because they'd found somewhere to buy. I laughed, and then analysed my response. Why hadn't I signed the rental contract weeks before, which would at least have committed them to paying a hefty deposit? It was so stupid of me. I should have been indignant and angry, especially having paid for and organised all those expensive shreddings and storings. But instead I let out a guffaw of pure happiness.

From then on I drove to the cottage almost every week, thrilled that it was still mine, and that the lovely garden was available for me to enjoy, snowdrops in winter, tulips in spring, hibiscus and hydrangea through the summer. I owe that army family a great debt: it was only because I nearly lost it that I realised how much I love our little cottage.

Now I'm wrestling with the thought of leaving my family home in London, my children being on the brink of finding their own flats with friends. Once again my rational and supportive accountant has no doubt that is the sensible thing to do. Of course I should sell it, realise the capital and put it somewhere safe so that I can live on the income. As the sometime-spokesperson for an equity-release broker, I know he's right. Moving on and out makes perfect sense. But how?

There are my children's paintings in every room. I watch the sun rise from my bedroom window. The imprints of dozens of birthday parties are almost visible on the garden lawn. Each spring is heralded by the explosion of white blossom on our cherry tree by the wall. Then there's the appalling, Himalayan task of de-cluttering every nook and cranny, decided what to do with the rocking horse, and my wedding hat. So when a charming lady approached me recently and offered a very fair price for the house, in spite of the gloomy forecasts declaring that property prices were about to fall precipitously, and although I'd always criticised little old ladies who hung on to homes far too big for them, I turned her offer down. That's the sort of idiotic, stuck, irrational person I am. My only excuse is that when she made her offer, and for one wild moment I thought I would accept, I didn't feel wealthy, or secure. I felt bereaved.

But even though I may not be able to bring myself to move out, I recognise I simply have to move on. Perhaps I should take lodgers, fill the house with friends and colleagues who need a room, and in return will share a pizza with me. Maybe I should convert the basement into a granny flat, or the top floor into a penthouse. Perhaps I should sign up to a marriage bureau, and start life all over again. As I sit stirring a cup of tea and making excuses to do nothing, I know, to my shame, that these life-changing decisions are completely beyond me.

I have a friend, a brilliant academic, who was widowed

about the same time as I was. Unlike me, within months she had sorted out her papers, her furniture and her pictures and moved out of the family home and into a flat, far more conveniently located. At about the same time she met a man of just the right age, suitable temperament, and they became an item. The odd thing is that I've never particularly thought of her as sensible or orderly, she's rather spiritual and fey. But, my goodness, when the time came to be decisive she let her head rule her heart. So, following her example, my advice to you would be, when circumstances alter and the wind changes direction, don't get stuck like me: move on. Take charge of your life, recognise how your wants and needs have changed, and alter your life accordingly. Be practical, but please don't ask me to follow your example. Moving on is simply not a skill I have ever mastered. I suspect I never will.

Chapter Six

A Woman's Place is in the Wrong

> *I am a woman, I am invincible,*
> *I am pooped*

Anon

The biggest adjustment we have had to make in the last seventy years or so has been right at the centre of our lives, in our very being. Our own core values as individuals and as a society have changed out of all recognition. One generation earlier considered that divorce and illegitimacy were shameful. 'Unmarried mothers' were punished with ostracism and poverty. It was tough on their children. Today, when England leads Europe in teenage pregnancy, and the papers are depressingly filled with stories of mothers with seven babies by five different men, it's still tough on the children. It comes as an unpleasant surprise to tough convinced radicals to discover that there are still loads of problems to resolve, and that some were actually created by the exciting social revolution we baby boomers have been living through. There is no doubt that when we first threw out the rule-books on behaviour and morals our parents had confidently handed down to us, we were sure that we would never need them, that we could draw exciting new maps for ourselves, and explore a brave new world.

Perhaps every generation believes they are pioneers. The first woman who offered a man an apple definitely did. We may think of women as the conservative gender, while men leap over traditional barriers, women close the gate and settle down inside. But when it comes to social revolutionaries, women can be just as fearlessly iconoclastic as men. Think of Boudicca. Queen Elizabeth I, whose intellectual supremacy brought unprecedented peace and unity to her country, enabled an extraordinary flowering of the arts. And so it goes. While Shaftesbury was liberating child slaves, Florence Nightingale was recruiting bands of young women to try and heal the horrors of war. Marie Stopes, Marie Curie, Germaine Greer, Naomi Wolf: they and their disciples leaped ahead and, thanks to their example, every twenty-five years or so the horizon slid backwards, and we all inherited more space to move, and build, and dream.

We baby-boomers have every right to think of ourselves as pioneers, too. Perhaps, like me, you were a student thirty or forty years ago. I was lucky enough to be accepted by a women's college, Somerville, at Oxford, and spent three life-enhancing years there from 1959 to 1962. Those were revolutionary times, and we knew it. The 'satire boom' was just beginning, *Beyond the Fringe* opened in the Edinburgh Festival in 1961, bringing to an end the age of deference when the establishment, be they prime ministers, judges or policemen, were thought to be above criticism. The disillusion when we realised they were as fallible and as corruptible as the rest of us was painful, but it had to come. We have only to remember what happened in Stalin's Russia and Mao's China when a great leader was idolised and criticism outlawed.

Many of us who were born in the 1940s and 1950s had conventional upbringings in our nuclear, heterosexual two-parent families. Dads went out to work and mums were housewives, and proud of it – wearing aprons to do the housework because it was genuinely hard, dirty work. I remember my mother's mangle and carpet-beater; at a push I could use them now. But there was a mould-breaking earthquake on the horizon, and we could sense that women were at the heart of it. After all, they had played their part in winning the war, something I was aware of as one of my aunts was in the ATS, Auxiliary Territorial Service (the army) and another drove ambulances into Belsen and Poland. When peace came there was no way they wanted to give up the challenges they had thrived on, so one aunt became a social worker and the other a probation officer. It meant a readjustment for men, too, of course; some found it easy, and still do, others opposed it, and eventually had to give in ungracefully. The post-war generation of middle-class young people began to regard higher education and a university degree as their right. Students being natural iconoclasts, the rules that had made the fifties stable suddenly felt stale and ripe for destruction. Right on cue, enter the sixties.

The sixties were enormous fun, for those of us who remember them. 'Swinging London' made Britain feel like the centre of the universe. The fifties' twin-sets were junked in favour of Mary Quant's mini-skirts, young men grew beards and pony tails, the quickstep lost out to Chubby Checker and the Twist, (with the current passion for ballroom dancing, it's back again now, a sweet revenge for chiffon and spangles) and the more politically motivated of us were marching against the bomb. I turned twenty with the new decade, and my friends and I prided ourselves that delicate English roses were turning into feisty tiger lilies.

It must have been tough for some of the women who taught us, whose lives had been so very different. I remember one summer's day a couple of unmarried female dons staring at us students picnicking on the lawn. How they disapproved of us. One of the history tutors, a tall bony woman with a bun at the back of her head and a wardrobe that consisted of grey and beige cardigans, was quite unable to teach a friend of mine: she was too disconcerted by my friend's blue eye-shadow. Those teachers belonged to a generation who had consciously chosen not to follow their mothers' path, stay at home, marry the boy next door and have babies. Instead they remained single, left home and became academics. It had been a difficult struggle for them: they were among the first women to obtain degrees and academic posts; perhaps they felt we didn't properly appreciate their achievement or their sacrifice, which may be why they didn't like or understand us. We had inherited the emancipation they had fought for, but we had it too easy, were too self-indulgent, had too many opportunities. We belonged to the first generation of 'liberated' women who expected to combine marriage, a family and a career. Maybe they despised us; perhaps they were jealous of us. Either way they couldn't cope with our desire to have it all.

But Dame Janet Vaughan, the principal of my college, was one of the people who led the way for us. She was a genuine pioneer, and a role model. A distinguished scientist, with power and influence in the world outside Oxford, she was one of the founders of the NHS, and she was also a married woman with a family. We used to talk with pride about her, and we were determined to follow in her footsteps, rather than those of the spinster tutors who lacerated us with their sarcasm, and forfeited our respect in the process. Not all our teachers were bitter and spiteful, but some were, and we wondered aloud to each other what on earth had made them become teachers when they so clearly despised their students, never thinking that perhaps they had had no choice when they were our age.

So we women were determined to live our lives without compromise. We wanted it all. And we managed it, for the most part. Although looking at my contemporaries, it's fascinating to see the way we have followed roughly the same route, if on slightly different paths. For example, my closest college friends and I all got married, and now, fifty years later, we have it in common that most of us have retained our original husbands, a feat in itself. Given that around half of all marriages end in divorce, I wonder what it is that gave ours such stamina. Maybe we have imprinted in our DNA a memory of the disgrace that divorce had meant to previous generations. Parents like ours (or most of ours) put up with incompatibility, and worse, for the sake of the children, and to avoid the poverty and social stigma of a broken marriage. Or perhaps it's because the age of deference was also the age of honour, when our word was our bond. We had made a public pledge to stay together till death us did part, so that was what we did. Or maybe we were just bright enough to pick the right men.

Even so, it has been a complex juggling act for us to try

to combine successful careers with parenthood, and we have each had to work out our own strategies. I was lucky to marry a man who so enjoyed fatherhood that he was happy to box and cox with me, making his documentaries during the down-time in my television series, so the children always had one or other of us at home. At least, that was the theory. I also compromised, choosing to make programmes based in London, rather than filming round the country, or the world. One of my friends, who was given the choice of a high-flying career in the civil service, turned it down for an academic job because she had married a university teacher and she wanted to be sure that wherever his work took him, she could follow. So now she's a professor, rather than the Dame she would have undoubtedly become, but as she turned out to be a highly gifted teacher, and had an extremely happy family life, it was clearly the right decision for her.

Not all my friends ended up living happily ever after. A few men of our generation decided to trade in the wives they'd had for twenty-five years in favour of newer, younger models. Why? Are there more divorces because it's so much easier? Or is it easier because more people want to divorce? Surely nobody would want to prolong a bitter, violent marriage. But my mother once told me that in her view, if you take out cruelty and addictions, the most corrosive element in a marriage is not sex, but money. Personally I think it's boredom. If two people can entertain each other, challenge each other and make each other laugh, it's possible to put up with bankruptcy, lies and adultery. But a monotonous marriage makes life unbearable. Look around any restaurant and you'll spot the couples who have been together so long they know every anecdote, can anticipate every thought and could probably choose each other's menus. The result is that they sit together in total silence, hardly even exchanging glances. Sometimes that's a companionable silence, but not always. It can be the warning signal that they no longer fancy each other's minds, and since attraction starts in the brain, that leads to physical antipathy too. And in this age of built-in obsolescence, when we no longer expect a dishwasher to last more than five years, it's hardly surprising that one or other partner starts to yearn for something, or someone, a bit more exciting around the corner.

I blame whoever designed the human psyche. Elephants and swans, after all, mate for life. But we humans are prone to suffer from that overworked phenomenon the 'mid-life crisis'. It's not sensible, but rational thought rarely has anything to do with it. A brand-new love affair is like yeast in the dough. It lifts the spirit, adds oxygen, boosts the sagging middle-aged morale. As our elderly reflections in the mirror fade to grey, admiration in a fresh pair of eyes can bring back the roses. It may be a long time since either of you felt attractive. From the anecdotes I've heard from friends, it seems that often when a man trades in his wife, it's preceded by long years of celibacy. Is that nature's contraceptive? Is it hormonally inevitable that we start to find each other unattractive, once we have explored each other's gene pool? It is striking how often childless couples retain the hand-holding sweet-talking sentiment of young lovers. Whatever the cause, feeling unwanted, physically or mentally, can be literally heart-breaking. So off he goes to the big-eyed girl who hangs on his every word, to whom his jokes are freshly minted and his grey hairs look distinguished. The wife who is patently bored with her mate and can't be bothered to disguise it, should consider the alternative. Boredom can be lethal to a marriage. And when it is, and the wife is left alone, life is suddenly not boring at all.

Of course the decision to divorce may be hers, not his. She may wake up each morning gloomily aware that the snoring, unshaven husband next to her is not the view she wants for the next ten, twenty, thirty years. Gradually she begins to recognise that he has become a stranger who irritates her. She minds his fatness, his obsession with football, she notices the fact that his breath smells, and that all his colleagues are smarter, brighter and richer. And she, too, begins to change. Women I know have found to their horror that their boredom has become frustration, and then anger, and finally a constant, nagging bullying. Some, when they recognise it in themselves, either leave or change. One friend, Diane, decided to part from her husband when their children were old enough to survive independently. She bought a flat, and started on a new degree course. At last she was going to become her own woman, instead of wife, mother, cook and organiser, the functions she had created for herself to keep the family going, rather than exploring her own talents. Just at that point she heard that her husband, now alone, had taken a young female designer with him to the South of France. That concentrated Diane's mind wonderfully. Her perception of him changed entirely. The tedious man who sat behind his newspaper reading the stock-market report was clearly wittier and more entertaining when he was with someone else. His middle-age spread and thinning hair must have seemed alluring to this new young woman, who could have found someone slimmer, younger and more muscular. My friend swallowed her pride and rang him. Perhaps they could try again. They did, but he, too, made compromises this time: he emerged from behind his newspaper and shared her delight in her academic achievements. Isn't it interesting how competition makes you value something, or someone, far more?

Another friend's life took a different course. Karen had married very young, but over the years had become intolerably bored with her husband. They had both been devoted parents, but their children had grown up and no longer needed active nurturing. Without those chores to fill their lives, the school runs, the family outings, the measles jabs and the Scout badges, she suddenly looked across the kitchen at her placid husband and realised they had nothing else in common. He was artistic, she was sporty; she loved travel, he enjoyed car maintenance. His calmness drove her mad; her volatility left him cold. One night she turned to him and said, 'Let's part. Let's not waste any more of the time we could spend happily with different partners.'

He had no idea such a cataclysmic suggestion was coming, and was devastated. His self-esteem had been clubbed to death, it seemed. But this story, too, has a happy ending. Both of them have now found new partners: he joined a car club and found a woman who shared his delight in classic cars; she was introduced to a businessman who could afford to take her on trips round the world. The children are pleased, because they can see both their parents are happy, and on friendly terms with each other.

All the couples I know whose marriages have come to grief, a hundred years ago would have tolerated anything, or found ways of concealing their differences, rather than endure the disgrace of divorce. But are we in the end happier than our parents' generation, who took their lumps because they didn't have the choice to opt for 'personal space'? According to surveys, our children here in Britain are among the unhappiest in Europe. Judging by the calls to ChildLine (the free national telephone helpline for children in danger or distress), much of that is due to discord and disruption at home. Be that as it may, unless the pendulum swings of its own accord, we can't force the clock to turn backwards, shove the budgerigar back into its cage. Women have a new role in society, and with it we have the opportunity to think of ourselves as potentially single units, even in our third age. Previous generations of women could only find an identity in marriage, or a few restricted trades and professions. The choice was never truly theirs. Now it is. Even if we are traded in late in life, we can and will, as the song says, survive. Provided, that is, we don't waste creative energy on keeping our fury alive. Easier said than done. A journalist once told me that a discarded wife under fifty can deal with her anger without allowing bitterness to consume her because she knows she still has plenty of time to find a replacement man. But if she is tossed aside over the age of fifty, she feels utterly furious that she has wasted her life on the wrong man, and now has very little chance of finding the right one. The problem is that by cherishing her new status as the wronged wife, she builds barriers around herself in her mind, and against the chance of a happy future. Obviously if she found happiness, or just a bit of fun, with somebody new she would lose the crown of thorns that gives her sanctity and makes her friends cluck with sympathy. And if someone did come round the corner with a gleam in his eye, he'd rapidly discover that he could never live up to what she's lost. Furthermore he might be wary of her, and he could be right. If hell hath no fury like her now that she's been scorned then she may *be* a bit of a hell-cat. Perhaps that was why the last man left, and maybe a new one should keep his distance in case he, too gets mauled. So I say, for everyone's sake, not least the children's, dump the fury and, as the Queen said, move on. The best revenge is to live well.

The truth is, marriage is no picnic. To make it work there will always be sacrifices on both sides. We, the generation who want it all, may try to keep all the plates spinning over our heads but, sure as heck, the moment we take our eyes off them one will come crashing down. Starting babies and a brand-new job in your twenties is like juggling alligators, brave but foolhardy. One way to simplify things a bit is to do what many successful women do and put off the whole idea of marriage and children until you are really established in your career. The downside of that, according to gynaecologists, is that female fertility drops sharply after the age of thirty. I was incredibly lucky to have had fifteen years of work before I married late, at thirty-seven, and even luckier to have had my three babies later, at thirty-seven, thirty-nine and forty-one. Readers with an investigative bent will notice that the wedding and the birth of my first baby were almost simultaneous and, yes, I was an elephantine bride, eight months pregnant. Cleverly I married in December and my daughter was born in January, so the two events happened in different calendar years. If my daughter ever wanted to convey the impression that I was a virgin on my wedding day, I suppose she could. Actually, of course, times and conventions have changed so completely that it doesn't matter at all to her, or me now. But when she was born thirty years ago, there was still a stigma attached to 'illegitimacy', and I wanted to get my daughter inside the fence of respectability, which is why I arranged our wedding in three weeks, and wore a dress bigger than most brides' marquees. Nowadays, I suppose, I might decide to have the baby first, and postpone the wedding until I could be radiantly slender. As it was, I was huge but happy.

As a wife and mother I started the way I meant to go on, with guilt. That is the besetting mood of the working mother. I was always in the wrong place: at home when I should have been at work, at work when I should have been at home. I missed my elder daughter's first steps, but I did see the pantomime she wrote. I took the children to school, but I couldn't pick them up at the end of the day. When I left for work, my toddler would rush up to her bedroom and position herself by the window, waiting for me to come home again. Our nanny used to coax her downstairs, 'Come and play. The time will go much faster that way.' She never told me, luckily, otherwise I would have dumped everything and rushed home.

I'm very struck by the fact that my daughters tell me now they have no intention of following my example. They would never put their careers before a family. They are not at all attracted by the idea of delegated parenting – nannies are too expensive, childminders too haphazard. They want to become full-time mothers at least for the earliest years of their children's lives, so somehow they will need to finance themselves. I wonder whether Dame Barbara Cartland, the romantic novelist, was ahead of her time when she suggested that mothers should be paid an income to stay at home and take on the most valuable and challenging work of all, bringing up their children. Maybe it would be difficult for society to afford to pay stay-at-home mums a salary, but in the long run it might be an investment. The alternative, where both parents work longer and longer hours, surely deprives children of their most precious asset, parental time.

I've never forgotten a boy who rang ChildLine about a very serious problem. I asked him why he hadn't told his mother. 'She's always so tired when she gets home from work,' he replied.

'Then why not pick a moment at the weekend to speak to her?' I asked him.

'She works in a shop,' he said, bleakly, 'So she's too tired at the weekend as well.' No wonder the shop-workers' unions are so opposed to all-day Sunday trading.

But if we were paid to spend more time at home with our children, would we know how to use it? So many of us seem to have lost the art of family life. TV programmes like *Supernanny*, and *Honey We're Killing the Kids* reveal chaotic homes, where the adults arrive back in the evening exhausted, the children have no bedtime or mealtime routines, the daily diet is frozen pizza and takeaway curry and chips. Parents and children lead completely separate lives, hunched over different screens in separate rooms. They don't possess a table they can all sit round together.

In those homes where family life has splintered, the

women never seem happier as a result. And yet they are very often the major bread-winner. As Mum watches the imported 'expert' trying to turn the family around and create order out of chaos, a great deal of the emotional burden rests on her shoulders. She has to make space in her life, and her heart, for the children. She has to offer Dad back half the power, a share in decision-making, if her working role has undermined him. Together they must begin to reinstate old-fashioned concepts, like family meals where they can all talk together, a regular bedtime, and Dad is encouraged to take his turn in reading bedtime stories. That is the only way, it seems, that everyone, Mum, Dad and children can feel confident that each one has a place in the family home which is theirs by right.

With time, even in the best-regulated and organised homes, a new element arrives to add additional burdens, the disabilities and vulnerability of old age. Our parents reach this often painful stage first, and most of us regard them as our responsibility. They may be fiercely protective of their own independence, often they are. But still we know how much we owe them, both as our parents, and as our children's grandparents. So having played their role as carers, maybe in their last years they will need caring for. 'Your son is your son till he gets him a wife, your daughter's your daughter the rest of her life,' the old saying goes. Usually the adult daughter is the one who copes, has to make sure she lives near enough to deal with disasters, like illnesses or accidents, is able to keep popping round to make sure important details are not forgotten, that meals are being eaten, and clothes are clean and warm enough. From baby to adult then back to dependent baby, that is humanity's journey if we live long enough, and our children will become the sandwich generation: they care simultaneously for their children and us, their parents. This is where we get what we deserve, it seems to me. The loving, generous parent gets the devoted son and daughter. The negligent or vicious parent gets the family who never visit – why should they? That may not always be the case. No doubt there are some selfish young people who repay years of care with callous disregard or exploitation. There have been hideous stories of middle-aged adults who cheat and rob their old parents and, rightly, are sent to jail when they are discovered. But for the most part children repay what they have been given and, difficult and tiring as it may be to look after a dotty old dear, are glad to, and feel guilty if they don't.

So here we are again as we face the prospect of our own old age, rightly or wrongly dealing with guilt, the prevailing emotion of the women who try to have it all. How will we eke out our savings so as not to become a 'burden'? How far should we de-clutter our lives, chuck out our treasures, so as to save our children the chores? Or, as people become more and more fascinated by their own family history, do we leave it all intact for them to leaf through and then feed into the shredder? And how will they judge us after we've gone? Did we find a brave new world for them, or will they decide we led them into a cul-de-sac?

My tutors, desiccated old spinsters as I thought they were, may have been more realistic than I realised, and perhaps we students were living in a dream world when we thought we could effortlessly do everything, take on every role. The current generation are wiser. A number of my college friends tell me their daughters, clever young women with university degrees, opted to become 'home-makers' while their children were young. The pendulum seems to be swinging backwards and, given women still have the freedom to choose, and if it benefits our children and grandchildren, perhaps that's no bad thing. That is often the fate of pioneers, to be contradicted by subsequent generations. The trick is not to be the first to have a good idea, but the second. So perhaps our sons and daughters will learn from our mistakes, and instead of trying to have it all, share it all between them. Shared bread-winning and shared parenting sounds eminently sensible. And if it works well, everyone, and above all our grandchildren, will be the happier for it.

Chapter Seven

The Secret of Eternal Youth?

> *Be careful of reading health
> books, you may die of a misprint*

Mark Twain

hile we're busily trying to recycle, save
waste and stop polluting our fragile
planet, nobody mentions the huge amount of
energy we squander on advising each other how to stay
young, healthy and fit. How many books, magazines, DVDs,
TV and radio programmes have preached at us and depressed

us? Every time you look up, some harpy is wagging her finger and instructing us to jog more, eat less, have less sex, drink less wine and, altogether, have much less fun. It's all counter-productive. As writer and broadcaster Ludovic Kennedy once pointed out, there's not much point in prolonging our lives by a few months if the effort makes us gloomier for years. And maybe it won't make us live longer anyway: those years will just feel longer.

So this chapter is designed to make you feel good about the way you have chosen to live, however that is. After all, you've had a good few years' experience, and if you're breaking the rules, that's your decision. What is the point of my telling you that smoking is dangerous? You know that already, you've been scolded a million times, and if you continue to smoke, that is the choice you've made. Equally, I reserve the right not to buy cigarettes for you, put ashtrays out for you or let you smoke in my home. That's my choice.

However, although I hope and assume that you are now happy in your skin, perhaps you have been noticing changes in your body over the years, some good, but others less cheering. We've talked in a previous chapter about the cosmetic changes. What about the more crucial alterations, the ones that may weaken us, or shorten our lives? Should we worry that we are beginning to get a bit breathless climbing hills and, if so, should we climb more gently? Do we care that our arms aren't long enough to hold the paper at a distance from which we can read it? What could or should we do about the beginnings of an inevitable decline? Is it really that inevitable?

Modern advances in medicine mean that some of these questions can be quite simply answered. For instance, you can climb down off the kitchen table, and stop trying to read a newspaper spread out on the floor when you've lost your glasses. In fact, you may even be able to throw your glasses away. Laser surgery can put right many of the eye defects our parents thought were irreversible. My grandmother had difficult cataract operations very late in life, when surgery had considerable risks, and she had to wait until she was almost blind, when the cataract was 'ripe', before it could be removed. My incipient cataracts were nipped out under local anaesthetic as easily as winking (literally) and replaced with silicone implants, which makes for interesting dinner conversation when I talk about my implants and am misunderstood.

And where eye surgery has gone, maybe whole-body therapy will follow. There may well come a time soon when all our cells can be given a quick shower with some new form of gene therapy, and our bodies can be seventeen again. (Though at seventeen mine was covered with 'puppy fat', horrible term, and my chin was overwhelmed with spots, so I wouldn't welcome that innovation.) Until then, how much can we do by altering our lifestyle to prolong, as the dog-food commercials put it, an active, healthy life?

The good news for us baby-boomers is that we have a

head start over the younger generations, at least when it comes to diet. According to health experts, we are exceptionally lucky, we who were born in the astringent years before supermarkets unleashed conspicuous consumption. It's quite difficult to look backwards down time's telescope and remember that in our war-baby childhoods, food was locally produced, eggs were free-range and vegetables were organic. Roast chicken was a Sunday treat, and our weekday meals of fish and vegetables were accepted as quite normal, where now they are imposed upon us as a 'de-tox diet'. Fast food was virtually unknown, no McDonald's, no KFC. Most food was slow, especially stews, in those pre-pressure-cooker, pre-microwave days. Before we get too nostalgic about the end result, at school I remember learning to make a very nasty stew out of 'scrag end'. I'm still not sure what part of which animal it was, but it was greasy, chewy and white. Fruit and vegetables were seasonal then, cabbage in the winter, strawberries in June, and exotic treats like mango and papaya never reached my local greengrocer in Cricklewood.

Then in the sixties everything changed. Since then we've enjoyed years of lavishness. We've grown used to eating red meat every day. Butter, cream and cheese fill our new fridges. We can have raspberries all year round, and look back on our early years as being unbelievably deprived. Throughout the seventies, eighties and nineties we ate and grew fat, until in the last decade the pendulum plunged backwards again, as the Puritans, no doubt, had divined it would. Now we've learned that the gorgeous sumptuousness of our middle years was lethal for us, and for the planet. Today's experts sternly tell everyone, especially the young, to cut back on the high-fat snacks and high-cholesterol treats they adore. Doctors predict epidemics of obesity, diabetes and heart disease unless our children and grandchildren mend their ways. But at least they reassure us baby-boomers that in our earliest years we were building strong foundations for a healthy old age.

Unless, of course, you choose to read the health pages of the tabloids and discover that although we are living longer than ever, these days, we also manage to be unhealthier. It appears that this is the age of allergies. We may have been pretty effective at discovering new chemicals, like antibiotics and statins, to conquer disease, but we've also been overwhelmed by other chemicals, which, it is said, have caused an epidemic of allergic disorders. Asthma and eczema, for instance, are on the increase, and everything from air pollutants to synthetic oestrogens has been blamed. And, thanks to the microscope, we now know about monsters like the dust-mite. To combat them we are instructed to deep-clean our mattresses, our carpets and our kitchens. Salesmen frighten us into buying special antiseptic wipes and machines to destroy the most persistent microbe. Our reward? We're told that over-disinfecting our homes is giving us cancer.

Personally I've grown allergic to all this advice. Day after day 'experts' in all the media tell us what to do for the best, healthiest, longest life. Much as we appreciate their concern, many of us would be even more impressed if the experts agreed with each other and stopped contradicting themselves. Red wine is bad for you, or is it good for you? Coffee is dangerous, or is it life-giving? And why on earth do these researchers who preach to us about what we should eat to keep cancer and heart disease at bay concentrate on foods like broccoli and blueberries? Please keep it real. Who can live on broccoli and blueberries? Try asking for blueberries on a train, or a plane, or at the sandwich shop on the corner. What's more, a headline in today's paper tells me I'm now eating too much fruit. What? How about the five different-coloured fruits and vegetables the Government tells me I have to cram into my mouth each day? It's enough to drive me straight back to the cheesecake, with or without a blueberry topping.

Are there any pieces of advice all the experts agree on? Certainly. If you want to live to a grand, fit, productive one hundred years old, become a nun. Gravestones in a cemetery in the West of Ireland reveal that even in the nineteenth century the sisters at the convent lived on until their late nineties. A researcher in Kentucky, David Snowdon of the Sanders-Brown Center on Aging, studied nuns in Minnesota and found an extraordinary plethora of centenarians. There are, of course, various hypotheses as to why this should be. It may be that God protects His own, or that life lived according to a regular routine, with set times to wake and sleep, pray and work, gives the body a rhythm it likes. Or perhaps it's the plain food, self-sacrifice, no smoking, no drinking, or (my least popular theory) no sex. That would be a step too far for many of us. Fortunately yet other researchers have dictated that sex into your nineties is obligatory if you want to keep everything working.

Not that that is an especially appealing idea. I once interviewed a ninety-year-old man who entertained ladies of all ages to tea. He supplied the biscuits, provided they accepted that the price was a bit of rumpy-pumpy with him. 'Don't bother to come round unless you want sex,' he said, and the whole studio audience groaned with revulsion.

But you don't have to be a promiscuous geriatric to keep the system moving. All the research shows that marriage is good for us. Some statistics suggest it adds seven years to a husband's life, and two to his wife's. Close friends and children also have a therapeutic effect – in other words, having people who care about us and keep in close contact is good for our health. Isn't it nice that serious, distinguished researchers are so committed to proving scientifically what we could have told them anyway?

Too much advice is contradictory, and too much of the rest is impossible to follow. I'm delighted that nuns survive so well, but following their example would be difficult for me, as a Jewish mother of three. It's great to know that marriage is good for you, but not much help if you're single.

Avoiding stress is sound advice, unless your partner is chronically ill, or your home is flooded. All we can do is pick the advice we like the sound of, and dump the rest. I'm always surprised by how many people choose the self-denying ordinances . . . at least, for a week or so. If you can keep it up for life, there is evidence that all the sacrifice may be justified: for instance, mice who are half starved live thirty per cent longer than normal. Many of us have tried that sort of masochism, with the cabbage soup diet, for example, or the only-proteins-beginning-with-P diet. The trouble with these drastic measures is that they set up such cravings. I've never really wanted Turkish delight until I was told I couldn't have it. And crash dieting followed by bingeing is notoriously bad for us.

If we seriously want to lose weight, the question is, out of the multi-billion-dollar diet industry filled with cons and swindles, what actually works? To try to find out, I tested all the most popular diets of the time on *That's Life!*. To provide a control group I added a spurious new 'diet'. I suggested to our team of dieters that they shouldn't cut down what they ate but before each meal they should nibble a carrot. And after six weeks my spurious diet worked better than any of the others. In fact, all our dieters lost some weight. This led us to believe that our would-be slimmers had succeeded with us after they had failed so often before because they had had to come into the studio every week, weigh themselves publicly and announce the result. Slimming clubs work in the same way: there is a weekly incentive to stick to a sensible diet, hence their success.

Why worry, anyway? Rubens proved that big can be beautiful. Mae West and Marilyn Monroe may have been size sixteen. The reason is that it's not just a matter of vanity or fashion: many of us feel that keeping fairly slim puts an extra spring in our step. We hate being a muffin-top, bulging over our waistbands. So, one of the unsung benefits of age for some lucky people is that at last they reach a steady, fighting weight. Having spent much of my sensitive youth unpleasantly plump, and hating it, I tried every crash diet I could find or invent and my weight yo-yoed around, as it always does when you starve, then binge in compensation. In desperation I gave up dieting completely and decided to eat only what I really enjoyed. From that moment I stayed at a stable weight, neither thin nor fat. What was more, I found I naturally steered myself towards fruit, vegetables and simple food.

It struck me while I was watching on television the wondrous Nigella sashaying around her kitchen, deep-frying Bounty bars and throwing cream, butter, chocolate and a bottle of wine into everything, in her usual lavish way, that after five minutes I had overdosed on virtual calories – like drowning in toffee. In my youth I would have watched all those cakes, pies and puddings, salivating. Not any more. It all looks far too rich for me, these days. I think it's because, with the years, one's taste changes. My children and I always agreed that one of the tragedies of life is that whereas I only allowed them to eat sweets on Saturdays, for the sake of their teeth (which are all perfect but do they ever thank me?), adults like me (and now them), who could theoretically eat sweets non-stop, rarely pick up a KitKat.

So, I've grown thinner with time. However, many of my friends have had the opposite experience, and find as the years go by that calories they could have gobbled down and burned off in their twenties gather lumpily around their hips in their fifties. Even if you do begin to carry a few more pounds than is fashionable, there is comfort in yet another survey, which has shown that overweight people actually live longer than those who are normal or underweight. Nobody is recommending obesity: carrying the equivalent of another person around the midriff overloads everything, heart, knees, the lot. But being pleasantly plump, it seems, gives us extra reserves to draw upon when flu strikes or the Norovirus hits us. Chubby people recover better. Also, thinness doesn't suit us over a certain age. Barbara Cartland, who died at ninety-eight, advised me that from the age of forty every woman has to decide between her face and her backside, because a slender rump inevitably means a gaunt face.

At a dinner recently, I sat between two famous beauties, one a bestselling author, the other an ex-model-turned-society-hostess, both so fragile they had bones like larks. From the back they looked like teenagers – they both wore the skinniest jeans available. But their bony cheeks and jawlines made them look like famine victims. Apple cheeks would have suited them far better but, no doubt, they were disciples of the Duchess of Windsor and believed you can never be too rich or too thin. To my envious eyes, they were both.

Dame Shirley Bassey celebrated her seventieth birthday in 2007, still glitzy, voice strong as ever, body toned and supple. I wish it was effortless; I know it's not. Shirley loves exercise. I don't. Every time I get out my trainers and sweatpants, I think about the exercise gurus who drop dead in the middle of a squash game or a jog, and put them away again. But the experts are unanimous that I'm wrong. The current view is that energetic exercise turns back the body clock ten years. If it makes you sweat, so much the better. According to *New Scientist*, Joan Smith Sonneborn, a biologist at the University of Wyoming in Laramie, says that stressing your body with exercise works miracles: 'I am seventy,' she says, 'and have the bone density of a thirty-five-year-old.' I certainly intend to follow her example, from a distance, when I get round to it.

I confess I have never experienced the rush of the happiness hormone, serotonin, which is supposed to reward an hour's weight-training or a healthy bike ride. My local hospital in London conducted an experiment that made me laugh all the way back to my sofa. They created an exercise programme for a group of older people, involving walking and light aerobics, and reported it did them the world of good, provided it didn't kill them. Their muscles strengthened, even their cognitive functions improved. However, it did kill some of them because they fell over, broke their hips and never recovered.

If you yearn for exercise but want to stay safe, personal trainers recommend swimming as the most effective way to tone the body, especially in a beautiful open-air pool in the South of France, or the warm waters of the Caribbean. I can't pretend that I've ever found my local swimming-pool an ecstatic experience. Those changing rooms, those showers, that smell of chlorine, the snap of Lycra around the thighs are not the most sensual indulgences in the world. The truth is that the more I exercise, the more bored I get.

The one sport I can wholeheartedly recommend is ballroom dancing. It improves your posture – a morning's tangoing is the equivalent of a ten-mile hike – and the music lifts the spirit. Indeed, listening for an hour or two to the music of your youth is entirely therapeutic. Download the tracks of the songs you enjoyed in your twenties, and suddenly you're twenty once more. And guess what, there's expert research to bear that out. According to *New Scientist*, the things that make you happy lengthen your life: for example, a bar of chocolate, or sitting in the sun with a glass of wine or beer, or falling in love. (I'm not going to depress you by pointing out that today's newspaper has just announced that even newer research seems to show that daily chocolate can give you brittle bones, and that the health-giving friendly bacteria in yoghurt can be harmful. Let's not go there.)

If you find all these contradictory messages make you feel stressed, never mind. The *New Scientist* article says that things that stress you out can also do you good, provided you are only stressed in moderation. This is an effect called 'hormesis', which scientists have tested by exposing yeast, fruit flies and worms to a little poison, radiation and heat. They lived for longer than usual, to the equivalent of a human's ninety years. To prove that a little stress can be good for us mammals, too, *New Scientist* quotes a survey of 28,000 ship workers who were exposed to low doses of radiation. To everyone's astonishment (and doubtless the huge disappointment of the no-win no-fee compensation lawyers), their mortality rate was 24 per cent lower than equivalent ship workers who had not been radiated. The reason is, scientists believe, that a little damage perks up the body, forcing it to give itself a shake and start repairing the injured bits, including areas that have worn out with the passing of time. So the enthusiastic keep-fit addicts we see stressing themselves on their walking machines might be right. We just have to be sure we understand how much is good for us, and how much is too much, so we can draw the line before the poison does serious injury.

There are more comfortable ways to achieve longevity. If you aren't inspired by the fact that nuns, radiated shipyard workers and poisoned fruit flies live longer than most, consider orchestral conductors as role models. Some of them carry on well into their eighties. Take six of the greatest: Toscanini retired at eighty-seven, von Karajan was still conducting until he died at eighty-one, Beecham gave his last performance at eighty-one, Solti gave his thousandth at eighty-five, and Boult bowed out at eighty-nine and Stokowski was still working when he died at ninety-five. All were travelling around the world, conducting strenuous concerts well past retirement age. Bus conductors, who only have a few miles on the average route to contend with, hang up their cap and badge far earlier.

What did the great men have in common with each other that made them so extraordinarily long-lived? First, status. Wherever they went in the world, travelling first class, of course, they were addressed as 'Maestro'. They were accustomed to being top dog. They dominated, took the lead and brooked no denial. That most pervasive and destructive form of stress, lack of control over your own life and the denial of any right to make your own decisions, was unknown to them. Everyone deferred to them: 'Yes, Maestro, of course, Maestro.'

Then they were cleverer than most of us. They commanded respect with a combination of charisma and outstanding intelligence, that special musical intellect, sharp and brilliant. But intelligence alone, alas, won't prolong anyone's life: look at the poet Keats, dead at twenty-six. Nor will musicality: many orchestral players are just as musical as those who conduct them, but they are not renowned for their longevity. However, there is a significant physical difference in their working conditions. Violinists and trombonists in the orchestra sit on their chairs doing what they are told. Unlike the *maestri* they can't spend their working hours standing on a podium waving their arms around. Think about it: conductors get their daily workout standing on the spot, without endangering themselves by power-walking or jogging and falling over. What could be better for lung capacity, load-bearing and muscular exercise? Why don't we all do that? We may not have our own pet orchestras to dominate, but maybe we should pretend, spend an hour or so conducting our favourite music in the privacy of our bedrooms in the morning. It may sound a little ridiculous, but who knows? It may well be better for us than pounding away in the gym, or going on a ten-mile trek.

Then there's sex. Without prying too deeply into the lives of these great men, the charisma of the *maestri* also meant that most of them had extremely active romantic lives, usually with very much younger women, which seems to have done nothing to shorten their lives. If it's a choice between being a nun or an orchestral conductor, I know which I'd choose.

What other factors promote a long, healthy, active life? It seems that location and vocation play their part. You will probably have noticed, as I have, that old people who spend the winter in Spain or Florida are relaxed and suntanned, and manage to miss out on the pneumonia and rheumatism that kill and torment so many elderly people in northern climes. Cardiologists famously retire to southern Italy or the South of France, so they can benefit from the 'Mediterranean effect', a diet rich in olive oil, which keeps their artery walls clear and smooth.

Personally, if I changed my location radically just to live a bit longer I would feel as if I was exiled from those I love. Instead, in my third age, I try to take winter holidays in the sun to top up my vitamin D, and at home I substitute olive oil for margarine and butter. Until, that is, the next scientific discovery proves that butter is better for me.

The idea of finding a vocation that sustains your interest and enlivens your life may be more practical, if exile abroad doesn't suit. It can happen at any age, for example, take the joy some of my friends have found acting as reading mentors or helpline counsellors. We don't always know how lucky we are, those of us whose education concentrated on the Three Rs. We assume everyone is literate, then are delighted to discover that the skills we take for granted are enormously in demand. I have visited an inner London school where the pupils speak thirty-two different first languages, but very little English. Many of the children have survived terrible traumas, war or imprisonment; they may be fearful and suffer nightmares and flashbacks. Some of us baby-boomers could offer a few hours a week that would make all the difference to children like them, not just providing English language teaching but also a caring eye. The challenge of ensuring the children speak, read and write fluent English is considerable but, of course, crucial for them. And it's a very special feeling to know that you have transformed a child's life.

These experiences can change your life, too. A cousin of mine found her vocation in her third age. A countrywoman with a farmer husband, she had always been an active member of her local Women's Institute. When he died, far too young, she was only in her fifties. She immersed herself in the WI and rose rapidly through the ranks, becoming a real power in the land, she, who had never had a career and was always modest and unassuming about her own ability. I was thrilled for her.

New mental challenges are not only good for our brains and souls, they may even add radiance to our funerals. There's nothing sadder than the empty church with only the vicar to say farewell to the coffin, but a crowded church for a centenarian is the evidence of a life fulfilled to the last.

The final piece of good news I have to offer in your pursuit of health and long life is, smile and you'll feel the benefit. Many studies have shown, unsurprisingly, that people with a positive, happy outlook last longer than those with a miserable personality. If you happen to feel sad at this moment, I apologise: no doubt this will only depress you more, but if it does, try this simple exercise. Force the corners of your mouth up. Forgive the Pollyanna-ism but the physical effect of smiling actually makes you feel happier. It has an additional side effect: a smile works as well as a face-lift, pulling up your cheeks and chin, and brightening your eyes. You must occasionally have caught sight of yourself scowling and noticed the ageing effect. So keep smiling.

On a really bad day, why not try a wonderful, breath-taking bout of laughter? I keep copies of Mel Brooks's *The Producers* and *Blazing Saddles* standing by for my three-in-the-morning blues. You might choose Billy Connolly or *When Harry Met Sally*. As a nation we idolise our opera singers and scream for our pop idols, but we love our comedians. Actors and singers may entertain or move us, but comedians make us happy, and they prolong our lives. So, no matter how grim the moment seems, whether you've just opened your latest tax bill or your daughter has run off with a drug-dealer, force yourself to sit down, draw the curtains, shut out the world, and watch something you haven't seen for years but you remember made you cry with laughter. Let yourself go. It's good for you.

And a final piece of health advice: follow the example of Queen Elizabeth II, and pick a parent who lived until she was over a hundred. You will have noticed that, these days, when you go to your doctor the first question invariably is, 'What age did your parents die?' There's a reason. The strongest medicine in the world won't do you as much good as strong genes. Of course, the Queen, fit, active and as popular as ever in her eighties, does a great many other things right. She doesn't smoke, she rides every day, she keeps regular hours and has a strong sense of duty. Add to that a very powerful family life and, according to butler Paul Burrell, apart from the official banquets, a taste for light, plain food: her idea of pleasure is a small plate of grilled fish in front of the TV. Also she knows where the next penny is coming from, which must alleviate the kind of stress many of us experience in our third age, and almost alone among the royals, she and Prince Philip have shared a very long-lasting marriage. She ticks every box.

So, accept the advice you like the look of and reject the rest because, sure as fate, along will come a new piece of research to contradict it. And if all else fails, the answer seems to be, if you want to stay healthy well past your bus-pass age and you can't be a nun or an orchestral conductor, be the Queen.

Chapter Eight

Whatever Turns You On

> *"Those who love deeply never grow old; they may die of old age, but they die young"*

Benjamin Franklin

W hen I made a documentary for the BBC called *Never Too Late,* based on a survey of several thousand viewers over the age of fifty-five, I expected it to paint a depressing picture of old age. After all, the only time most newspapers feature older people is when they are the victims of crime, poverty or injustice. The battered face of a pensioner, mugged for the few pennies in her pocket, is a familiar sight on the front page, not because it is a common event, most victims of violence are young men in their early twenties, but because it will produce outrage in the readers. The other journalistic stereotype is the tragic old person who dies alone in a freezing cold flat, deserted and unable to pay for heating. Also not a common occurrence, but once again, a story guaranteed the front page because it is so shocking. But the older people who took part in our survey didn't fit these stereotypes, so for a while we doubted its veracity. Was it just because viewers of BBC1 were more affluent, or middle-class, or in denial about the tragedy of their lives? But the more we read, the clearer the picture became. This was a story of older people enjoying themselves.

'Are you living alone?' we asked.

'Yes,' many replied. 'Because we choose to.'

'Are you bored?' was another question, and you can imagine how a teenager would have replied.

But the over-fifty-fives said, 'Absolutely not.' They told us that through the years they had come across so many possibilities they hardly had enough time to explore them all. How could they possibly get bored? At that time the ratings boffins in the television industry scorned the older audience, 'because they'll watch anyway, we don't need to put ourselves out for them'. Obviously they hadn't read our survey or they would have discovered that the older people who had taken part in it were not only busy but discriminating. Don't show them a lazily thought-out 'reality' show designed simply to show drunk people swearing at each other. They'll certainly not watch that. Funnily enough, TV audiences throughout this period were dropping like a stone. But the boffins who had turned their back on the elderly didn't ask whether they were on the right course: they'd got themselves stuck in a mind-set that the only audiences worth having were the young, and they went on frantically chasing the sixteen- to twenty-four-year-olds with programmes like *The Big Breakfast*, and all the 'mean TV' creations. At one stage the BBC lifts had '16–24' stickers on them, just to remind all the staff who their targets were. Every time I got into one I couldn't suppress a snort of contempt.

Why make adolescent TV, specifically designed to alienate a mature audience? Why not do what I had been trained as a programme-maker to do, and go for the broadest appeal possible, setting out to attract the kids and their grandparents? No, said the boffins, we must target particular hard-to-reach groups, like Essex boys who are addicted to motorbikes and lager. (Sorry, Essex readers, if that's libel, but it's literally what I was asked to do when I was making my daily talk show. Obediently I invited a few into our studio audience, and there they sat, legs wide apart, looking bored and mystified, and clearly terrified that some of their mates might recognise them there.) That was the era of the so-called 'tribes' theory, when the BBC brought out a huge bible describing the 'tribes' of Britain as if it were a study by anthropologists. Actually it was invented by jumped-up marketeers, who may have been wizards at selling cake mix, but knew nothing about entertaining television audiences. Fortunately along came blockbusters like *Strictly Come Dancing* which blew their crazy theories out of the world's windows by proving that you could reach the whole family with a great show. Hooray.

If only the boffins had taken the trouble to research older viewers before writing them off, they would have discovered a busy section of the population who were avidly pursuing their dreams. This myth that older people will watch anything is not only patronising, it's wrong. It's the teenagers who can't sit for a second without a machine to entertain them. Their grandparents have no time to glue themselves to the TV screen. Have they always wanted to create a little paradise in their own backyard? Now at last they have time. Have they long been fascinated with antiques? There are plenty of books and courses, and a loft full of knick-knacks to practise on. What about water-colour painting? Or joining a book club? Or perfecting one's cookery skills or, indeed, ballroom dancing, or having a gap year, like our lucky grandchildren, and roaming the world? That was what our survey revealed that this age group was up to, provided its members had a few savings. Obviously some didn't, and for them the state pension allows very little room to indulge any dreams – sheer survival is difficult enough. But many could, and did.

My own third age has been my age of opportunity, not because I'm a television fat cat, but because I have a far more precious asset: I have time. I've leaped off the conveyor belt. These days, when someone sweetly and rashly offers me a job presenting a programme live every week, I say, thank you, but no thank you. There's too much else to do. And wherever I go I find retired people doing exactly what I'm doing: making the most of the moment. A retired couple I met recently in one of the furthermost Cook Islands were about to go off skiing ten days after they got back home to Cheshire. They were happily spending the kids' inheritance, and enjoying every moment.

There are other delights nearer home. I admit I'm lucky: I've gleaned some advantages that not everyone can call upon from a forty-year career in broadcasting, such as an invitation to join *Strictly Come Dancing*. I had watched the first series, mesmerised. Not just because it's beautifully produced, which it is, but because nobody could fail to be impressed by the amount of sheer hard work the celebrities put in, month after month, to try and keep up with their professional partners. I remember being interviewed by Natasha Kaplinsky, the news presenter, soon after she had won the first series. I congratulated her, and asked, as everyone now asks me, 'Are you still dancing?' She blenched, and shook her head. Now I understand why. It's not just a matter of five minutes here and there, it's hours of work, every day. While you're booked for the show, it takes over your life, and Natasha stayed to the finals which, clever girl, she won. But even she, glamorous and graceful as she is, had to work her elegant backside off to get there, and once it was over, she came back with relief to real life.

But when I asked her that stupid question, I had no idea how focused and determined you have to be to ballroom-dance to her standard. After all, I already had a little experience. Exactly how little, I had yet to discover. All I'd done was learn a 'social' version of the waltz and the quickstep when I was fourteen, dancing with my cousin Roger, both of us taught by two delightful sisters whose busts got badly in the way when they whirled me around the floor, pretending to be men. But, still, we soldiered on, and then I spent some years being pushed around various dance-floors by embarrassed young men until rock and roll came in, and everyone let out a sigh of relief, let go of each other, and did their thing, wiggling or waving or both. Up to then I'd thought I was ballroom-dancing, but I now know I was just 'social dancing', a different thing entirely.

When I was introduced to my partner, Anton du Beke, I admitted to him that, as a dancer, I have a couple of handicaps. First, I have very long feet. Have a look at the professional dancers in the show and you will see that the women have enchanting little toes. Not me. When God made me, He built in a pair of skis. My second problem is a total absence of muscle memory. My mother used to say that I didn't learn to walk until I was eighteen months old. I was a fat toddler, so it was assumed that that was the reason. But now I think it was because it took me months longer than anyone else to learn how to put one leg in front of the other. And I had to learn far more than that at the age of sixty-four for the show.

But un-ideal as I was for poor Anton, I wholeheartedly recommend the process of learning. For one, it vastly improves your posture and stamina. What Anton did was straighten my spine, and encourage me to throw out my chest. Recently I had begun to stoop. I used to watch record-ings of myself presenting my talk show, scuttling around the studio with a hump. It wasn't a spinal disability, it was terrible posture. Even as I write this I instinctively straighten up and lengthen my neck, the way Anton taught me. You will have noticed Bruce Forsyth sometimes talks about 'lifting the diaphragm'. Anton taught me that, too. He insisted that I squash the underwire of my bra into his manly chest.

If you haven't got a manly chest handy to squash into, you can take up the position on your own. It's great for improving family photographs. This is what you do. Stand in front of a full-length mirror. Lift your diaphragm. Drop your shoulders. Lengthen your neck. (Keep breathing, otherwise you may have perfect posture but you'll also be purple.) Pull in your stomach so that it touches your spine. Now look at yourself. I bet you've dropped ten years and ten pounds. For perfection, and to show off, ladies, drop one hip and put your hand on the hip you've dropped, (not the other one – that just makes you look like a fishwife about to start a brawl: the hand on dropped hip lengthens and slims your waist). Men should probably not put their hands on either hip. Instead put one hand in a trouser pocket, which looks more like Cary Grant and less like Larry Grayson. But it's your choice.

Besides posture, I learned the back whisk, and the fan, and the chasse, and how to smile and fall over on command. When asked to define my style, Anton described it as 'random'. How right he was. Neither he nor I ever knew, if he let go of me, which way I'd head off. Thank heaven I only lasted till week three. If I'd gone on, I would have had to do the Paso Doble, in which the lady has to pretend to be a matador's cape. I suspect I would have been less the Cape of Good Hope, and more Cape Wrath. However, I wouldn't have missed a second of the months I spent learning the waltz, the rumba and the tango: I lost weight, my waist dropped several inches (they're back now, alas), and Anton and I still have dinner and laugh together, although we no longer dance. I think he can't stand the stress of never knowing where I'm going. But even without Anton I thoroughly recommend that you pop round to the nearest classes and have fun. As I said in chapter seven, it's much the most enjoyable form of exercise, in my view, and it's good for you in every possible way.

Older dancers often have an innate grace, because in their youth they put in hours of practice at the local palais, and they know what they're supposed to be doing. Unlike most other forms of exercise, you're meant to trot round in the arms of someone of the opposite sex, which is often an advantage. And to answer your question before you ask it, I have no idea whether one thing will lead to another. In Anton's case it certainly didn't with any of his partners, but there is plenty of gossip about other couples, and it is tempting to assume that the ones who look deep into each other's eyes and whose legs are blissfully entangled are more than just dancing partners. You may say what you like, I couldn't possibly comment, but Anton did once tell me that couples who bonk never dance so well afterwards. Mind you, actors say that about stage lovers, that you can only portray passion if you're not doing it in life. Tell that to Elizabeth Taylor and Richard Burton, or Laurence Olivier and Vivien Leigh, or Katharine Hepburn and Spencer Tracy, or – shall we stop there? Circumstances clearly alter cases.

Gardening is also a skill older people acquire over time: they become more and more accomplished and knowledge-able with age. After all, apart from the decking some of the television gardeners imposed on us because they only had a day in which to transform a garden (I suppose we should think ourselves lucky that the producers didn't insist on concrete), it takes years to learn how to create a garden. You have to discover that the quality of the earth matters so much, and the direction of the sunlight. Then there are the vagaries of the different plant species, and the predatory habits of slugs and greenfly. From there you move on to matters of taste: are you organic, or chemical? Do you prefer the bright colours of summer bedding or the subtle greens of shrubs? None of this can be absorbed in a few months, so look round any garden centre and you'll find plenty of customers of fifty-plus, and if the company is enlightened, many of the sales people too, hired not out of pity or obligation but because time has turned their fingers green. I always loved flowers, even as a child; my grandmother taught me they were precious. The only time I ever remember seeing her angry was if we picked a wild flower, a bluebell or a primrose, and let it drop without taking it home and putting it in water. She showed me the flowers in her herbaceous border, and discussed the mysterious loss of fragrance in so many of them, bred for showy blooms without the scent. She would bury her nose in a rose, or 'cherry pie', and lament the loss.

Now the growers have learned the error of their previous ways, and have bred fragrance back in. 'Scent is the soul of the rose,' as my old friend the comedian Cyril Fletcher used to tell me. He was the second great gardening influence of my life, having created garden after garden for his beloved wife, Betty. He told me it took seven years to establish a garden, and he took enormous pride in the fact that he had planted every flower and shrub himself. I certainly can't claim the same. At the time we met, although I loved plants, my fingers were notoriously brown. I could walk past a plant and kill it. Over the years, I'm delighted to say, that has changed. Partly that's Roy's influence.

Roy Hayter trained as a gardener when he left school at the age of fourteen. He learned how to prepare the soil and enrich it until no plant could resist it. He could dig and hoe until he was in his mid-eighties. His blond hair is lightened by Hampshire sun and rain, and he speaks with a light New Forest burr. When we met I knew nothing. I liked rabbits and deer, while now I would shoot them with my bare hands if such a thing were possible. I had two acres to play with around my cottage, land that had been a tussocky track from the fields to the farm it once was. Apart from a pretty little front garden and a few fruit trees that was it. I had great plans. I wanted a herbaceous border like Granny's (and I still want one twenty years later). It took me years to realise why. I didn't understand until Roy taught me that plants have minds of their own, and if you try to coerce them into growing somewhere they hate, they will glare at you, keel over and die. But it was a rare failure. Watching Roy plant a seedling born in the local nursery, or taken from his greenhouse, was like seeing a talented nanny tucking a newborn baby into a cradle. There'd be ample space for the roots to stretch and spread, the soil would nestle up to the stem, and you just knew it was happy.

Once I hired some lavender growers to create a new bed

for me, and Roy arrived too late to inspect their work before they left. He scornfully lifted one of the little weaklings out of their new home, to reveal pot-bound roots as distorted and cramped as a Chinese concubine's feet. This was not the work of someone who loved and respected gardening, as Roy did. The men came back with new plants, this time working under Roy's sharp inspection. He was very patient with me. When we met he also worked for a local builder with very different views from mine. I loved the fact that local wild flowers, the native bluebells, primroses and even, bless the day, a cowslip or two would slip past the hedge and take root in my gravel paths. Roy's other employer, the builder, wanted anything unplanned or irregular instantly removed. For him, Roy had to dig up every daffodil at the end of each spring, and replace them with thousands of summer bedding plants, the kinds I least liked, the busy lizzies and the French marigolds, bright and sturdy, standing in geometrical straight lines. I love the more temperamental Edwardians jostling in my beds, the Russell lupins, delphiniums and blowsy poppies. How Roy survived his schizophrenia between his two gardens, I don't know, but he managed. And for me he created the perfect blend between the formal style of the water-lily pond and the groomed lawns, and the hippie romantic arches dripping with white roses, lilies swaying in the long grass.

As time went by and my children grew up they needed less space on the lawn to play French cricket. (Remember

French cricket? Do children play it now, protecting their legs with a cricket bat as tricky bowlers try to fool them, making the ball swing round to tap their ankles? We loved it.) So when they no longer needed their grassy playground I began to fill the swathes of lawn with little streams and ponds, not realising what hard work it would be to battle with the slimy algae that filled them every time Roy's back was turned. Then, fool that I was, I asked for a vegetable patch, and Roy made one for me. Peas, raspberries, new potatoes, sweetcorn, all did as they were told and grew magnificently for him.

Magpie-like, I would steal other ideas from the gardens Desi and I visited. Rhododendrons from Edmund de Rothschild's magnificent park in Exbury. White roses clambering through my apple tree, as they do at Sissinghurst. I even tried for an 'orchard', a little group of fruit trees wedged between two hedges, where they had no light and the soil was tired and barren, so that didn't work either. I have tried over and over again to sprinkle my two acres with poppies, and they came up one year, a fabulous mixture of pinks, oranges and crimson, but only that once, never again. I've seen a wisteria I'd love to plant there; its black, twisted boughs enlace each other from ground to rooftop and cover the side of a tall Georgian house with pale mauve blooms, but even Roy couldn't make our wisteria climb that high in less than a hundred years. But usually when I asked for the impossible, Roy would laugh at me and try to make it happen. Astonishingly often, he achieved miracles. I used to marvel at his eyesight. Well into his seventies, Roy could spot the tiniest bud on a twig I'd thought was dead, or an aphid where no pest should be. Then tragedy struck us, as unfairly as it usually does. ('Don't grumble that life's unfair,' Cyril Fletcher once told me. 'Nobody ever said it was going to be fair.') Roy's sight began to fail. He had developed macular degeneration, the most common form of age-related blindness. At first he persevered, although the cruelty of the disease is that it knocks out the very centre of one's sight, the most necessary part of all. But soon it became clear he was going to have to retire. I still ask his advice, and he is as caustic as ever about those who never had the training that make him such a wonderful gardener.

For me he is living proof that a great gardener is like an oak tree: you need to start with a good, strong acorn, but then it must live through years of sun, rain and fresh air if it is to achieve its full potential. Which reminds me: Roy found an oak seedling in his vegetable patch, carefully uprooted it, potted it up for a season or two, then planted it next to the stile into the next-door field, a very unpromising position on a clay ridge, but somehow he persuaded it to flourish. Now when I need to pull myself up over the top wooden step it offers its branch to assist me. Gardening is strenuous, but if you haven't the muscles to lift a spade or a fork, there are other rewarding skills to acquire, if you have the taste for them. There used to be a lovely programme on day-time television (at the time of day they put on all the incontinence-pad and stair-lift advertisements so you know who they thought would be watching) about learning water-colour painting. The wonder of that kind of art is that it's a constant challenge. You have to work extremely fast, you mustn't make any mistakes, and you learn how to use the white-paper background as your light source. It's extremely technical, but spontaneous at the same time. Perhaps, like me, you love water-colour pictures – my walls are full of them. I adore the translucency, the subtlety. It's like having extra windows to let in the light.

So, in my late forties I went on a weekend water-colour course with Professor Sir Roy Calne (the transplant surgeon who operated on little Ben Hardwick), and a group of his surgeon friends. Surgeons enjoy using their hands, for obvious reasons, and often do a lot of DIY at home. So, if you're wondering whether your surgeon's up to it, why not call round and have a look at his fitted cupboards? Anyway, it was an eye-opener, once again. Like ballroom dancing and gardening, I'd had no idea how ignorant I was until I tried it. Now, whenever I go on a cruise, which is as often as possible, I sign up for the water-colour course.

Travel is another hobby that improves with age. You may have had family holidays in France or Italy, but I bet you haven't in Rarotonga or Machu Picchu. And you don't have to be a millionaire to explore the world in comfort (though it does help: a private jet saves you all that unpleasantness at airports, I'm told, those hours of check-in and security that make flying a real torment, like staggering your way round an army assault course) because there are some fabulous deals to be had on cruise ships. The most often-asked question from one cruise-ship passenger to another is, 'How much did you pay?' and the second most asked is, 'How big was your discount?' Cruise companies want, above all, to fill their ships so that they can make money on our coffees, cocktails and on-shore tours. If you book at the last moment, and don't care about port-holes or balconies, you may find yourself down by the engine-room but you'll still be going to wondrously exotic places and letting the ship take the strain.

There are yet other ways of seeing the world if you're on a limited income. The father of a friend of mine was widowed in his eighties, and his family worried greatly about him. They needn't have. It turned out that he was an outstanding bowls player, so in his eighties he travelled the world with his local team, the guest of a dozen gorgeous places like South Africa and New Zealand. However, if you are looking to augment your income so that you can fulfil the dreams of your youth, let me pass on one disappointment to you. Don't rely on selling your family heirlooms and making a few thousand that way. It's amazing how quickly a treasured antique turns into a pile of junk once an expert sets eyes on it. My mother had cut-glass tumblers she treasured, and silver, and nice old wooden furniture. After she died, the expert we asked to value it all turned up his nose at the lot.

When he saw my face fall, he sympathised. 'You're not alone. Shows like *Antiques Roadshow* make everyone think they've got a fortune stowed away in the loft. But the truth is you probably haven't. This stuff has no value at all, because nobody these days wants to buy a cut-glass tumbler that'll cost you thirty pounds to replace when you drop it. They'd rather buy one new for a fiver. And most of us haven't got a butler, so cleaning silver is a bore, unless you're an Oxford college and it's Georgian. And, of course, brown furniture is right out.'

I looked at the rosewood dining-room table he was sniffing at. 'Why is brown furniture out?'

'Four letters. IKEA. It's all chrome and glass, these days, cheap, practical and minimalist.'

I showed him a little walnut table Mum was especially fond of, with an inlaid pattern of a flower on the top. Sadly, she had stood a plant pot on it for years, and water had damaged the veneer badly. 'Cost you more to repair than it's worth,' he said.

'Not to me,' I told him, and kept it. I learned from that experience that you might as well hang on to anything with sentimental value because that's all it's likely to have. You may be the illegitimate heir of a duke with a passion for Constable or Reynolds, and have some fabulous portrait hanging in your loo, but most of us, it seems, haven't. If you'll forgive that crumb of bad news, you must admit that the rest of the story is very cheerful indeed. The point is that by now you will have a number of interests you never had time to pursue before and now, at last, you have, so let your butterflies fly, and your dreams may well be in reach. If so, don't hang about, go out and enjoy. You're only young once, thank goodness, so now that's over and you're in your prime. Make the most of it.

Chapter Nine

Sex, Lust and Love

> *'Tis better to have loved, lusted*
> *and lost, than never to have loved*
> *and lusted at all*

O nce upon a time in the 1990s I was making a television awards show called *Hearts of Gold*. One of the regular items was a hidden camera test we called 'The Good Samaritan Survey'. The theory was that we would set up a dilemma in the street, like an old lady who had dropped a precious birthday cake, or whose cat had somehow got stuck in a chest of drawers in a skip, and see how many passers-by would come to the rescue.

One memorable dilemma we invented was the plight of the bride whose fiancé's best man had arrived too drunk to do his duty at the ceremony. We cast as the best man a young actor from one of the Australian soaps, who had no problem at all thinking himself into the part. Another actor played the bridegroom, again easily sorted. Then the question arose, who should play the bride? 'I'll do that,' I said, and was quite unprepared for the naked horror on my young male producer's face. He tried to cover his spasm of disgust by pretending it was because he feared I'd be recognised. But I knew the truth. It was the idea of a fifty-five-year-old bride that gave him the heebie-jeebies. In the end we found an almost opaque veil for me to wear, the Australian best man sat sprawled outside the register office, clearly comatose, and a passing trombonist agreed to take his place, dressed in black tie (which we supplied) with his own jeans and trainers. He took on the role nobly, including comforting the bride, who was sobbing beneath her veil, and trying to pacify the mother-in-law (an actress who specialised in playing formidable ladies), who was understandably outraged. Whether or not the trombonist was appalled when I revealed myself I don't know – if he was, he concealed it well. But my producer's response made me realise, if I'd ever had any doubts, how repulsive the young find the idea of old people coupling. Romantic love, fine, provided everyone recognises that it's a pure, platonic thing. But anything involving physical contact between the over–fifties? Yuck. So it's best to keep from them the fact that wrinkles and rheumatism don't automatically mean the death of hormones: middle-aged people can still enjoy sex. Indeed, the newspapers are full of the fact that fifty-year-olds are becoming a real problem in exacerbating the spread of sexually transmitted diseases because they are unused to safe sex and are inclined to change partners in what used to be called a promiscuous manner. Time is running out, they know, and any new encounter might be their last, so on with the dance.

While not advocating unsafe indiscriminate sex, I do understand why love-making is still important even when we're middle-aged and it's clearly not for procreation. I've no idea what it feels like to have a male orgasm, but female orgasm puts a smile on your face and in your heart. It's literally life-affirming. So it would be sad to think that just because we aren't as supple as we once were, nor as acrobatic, physical love is denied to us. In any case, I'm told there are ideal positions for older lovebirds who can no longer touch their toes or see their feet, which I'm sure you can look up on the Internet, if you wish. Recently I was attending a meeting with a very senior ITV producer whose current morning chat show was running on the huge screen behind her. Riveting as our conversation was, I kept being distracted by the sight of a portly elderly woman crawling into position on top of a man on a bed. After a while I had to ask, 'What is that?'

'A very important item about how to have good sex if you're old or disabled,' she said piously. To which the response is, whatever your age, the way to have good sex is in private, not on mid-morning television. Nor, I'm afraid, in this book, not because I'm particularly prudish but because I doubt my own expertise. I may have tried positions one to four, I may have heard about positions five to nine, but after that my imagination and experience give out. So for further information, again, I recommend the Internet.

Love, though, is easier to discuss because so many people have talked openly to me about the ways they found love, or lost it, or both, in their later years. And it's clear that lust and pain played a great part in it. I know of one illustrious writer, Poppy, who made a fortune writing romantic historical novels. Unexpectedly, when she was sixty, she was brutally thrown aside by her sculptor husband, Dan. Given his cruelty, her friends watched with satisfaction as he was abandoned in his turn by the model for whom he left home, who took his money and found another sculptor to immortalise her. Poppy was far too proud and hurt to take him back, even though it would have been practical to do so. There were so many simple domestic challenges she couldn't tackle by herself. Half the lightbulbs in the house were miles out of her reach. The wood for her open fires needed chopping, and carrying into the house. The tumble-dryer kept breaking down. Fortunately, a family Poppy had always known well lived across the road; their children had played with hers, gone to the same school, and so on. Their eldest son, Simon, now in his twenties, popped over from time to time, at his mother's suggestion, to check that Poppy was coping. On one pop-over he found her in tears over her misbehaving Aga. He put his arms round her. Their eyes met. It was a scene straight out of one of her novels. Knowing how furious his mother would be, and given there was a thirty-two-year gap between their ages, they kept their love affair secret, and when they eventually got married, the ceremony was in Tahiti with nobody from either family present. That was fifteen years ago. She is now seventy-five, he is forty-three, and they seem perfectly contented still.

The problem is that they are extremely isolated, because neither his friends nor hers can cope with what they perceive to be a grotesque mismatch. His mother still can't forgive them. Her children refuse to meet them both together, though she does occasionally see her grandchildren, on carefully stage-managed treats, like a trip to a pantomime or a theme park, without Simon being there. I asked him whether it was difficult to keep their relationship going with so many obstacles to overcome. 'No,' he said. 'We're soulmates, we always have been.' Poppy beamed at him. 'And, of course, we have masses of sex,' she said.

Beryl, from Newcastle, was an incurable optimist. To cheer herself up after a messy divorce when she was sixty-six she had gone on a safari holiday to Africa, and met a young Maasai warrior who was giving a dance display. I have watched similar displays, and they are impressive, the immensely tall young men in red robes jumping vertically, their clubs in their hands. Beryl was so impressed she asked James, then nineteen years old, to have a drink with her. It started a journey that led him back to Newcastle with her. When I met him he was almost completely silent. Beryl did all the talking. Looking at them sitting side by side, holding hands, it was difficult to know if one was exploiting the other, or whether they were in a dream world. How could it possibly work out for them? Even if she was rich in his eyes, by British standards they were on the bread-line. They lived in a tiny flat, he was lonely and bored, he found the language difficult and the freezing winters really uncomfortable. I was reminded of poor Pocahontas, the Native American princess, who saved the life of Captain John Smith, fell in love with another of the colonists, returned to England with him and almost immediately died, probably of smallpox. It can be fatal to be transplanted, even for lovers. However, in spite of her friends' and family's advice, Beryl was adamant that the Home Office was sure to recognise true love when they saw it, and that James would be allowed to stay and work in England. But what could he do? Stack supermarket shelves? That would be a huge step from entertaining tourists in the village he came from. That story ended sadly: James was denied permission to stay by a stony-faced Home Office and, left alone in Newcastle, Beryl had once again to face reality. She was an elderly woman who had made a fool of herself, and might never find another mate.

It's a tough message to have to grasp. A friend runs a hotel in the Caribbean. She recruited a very competent manager from a hotel in Wales, Dianne, a middle-aged woman who had never married and had long ago settled into a single life. Trinidad changed all that. The head cook in the hotel was a handsome young Trinidadian called George, with a cheeky smile and an engaging sense of humour. He began to flirt with Dianne. Nobody before had said her eyes were gorgeous, or that her greying hair was lovely, or that her rotund body was sexy and voluptuous. All women should hear such things, but many never do. Dianne was seduced. She started to wear makeup, bought herself some brightly coloured dresses covered with hibiscus and humming-birds, she sang around the hotel the lilting calypso love songs she danced to each night with George when the hotel guests were safely tucked up in bed. It's easy to ridicule her naïveté; certainly her friends warned her not to believe the sweet things George was telling her.

Then, when the hotel was at its busiest, she told my friend she was going back to Wales for a short holiday. Because she was such a reliable manager, and good staff are hard to find, my friend agreed. On the morning after she'd left, the guests were pounding the tables for their breakfast but there were no eggs or bacon to be had. George was in the seat next to

Dianne on the plane flying home. Once there she was determined to marry him, and she did. But as soon as they had convinced the Home Office that it was a genuine love-match, and the ceremony was over, George changed. Instead of the constant laughter, there were only frowns and complaints. Dianne tried desperately to please him, but nothing worked. She found another job in a local Welsh hotel, working very long hours, but when she returned home late at night, George was out, and sometimes didn't return all the next day. In the end Dianne threw him out, and he disappeared. She had served her purpose.

Desperation can blind a mature, intelligent woman to reality. Rebound can be just as dangerous. Laura is a fashion designer, one of the top in her field. Some years ago she was widowed, her husband Philip finally succumbing to a long, painful illness. They had had an enviable partnership: they made each other laugh, they supported each other in hard times. When he died she was distraught, and to numb herself from the agony and loneliness she began to work harder than ever. Those of us who watched her grief worried that she hadn't given herself a moment to allow the sorrow to surface. Then, on a working trip to Belgium, she met Chris, a very successful businessman from Leeds, also in the fashion industry. They sat next to each other at the obligatory trade presentations and talked together about everything, fashion, politics, religion, their families. When they took the Eurostar back he insisted that they share a taxi to have tea together in one of the big, glossy hotels in Park Lane. Tea became supper, and still they talked. They parted at three in the morning, and she found herself dreaming for the first time in many months of a possible happy future. It was a delight to see how she changed in the next few weeks as the affair progressed. She walked as if she was dancing, her eyes shone, the pain and anxiety left her face.

Alas, Chris was not as unencumbered as he had seemed. He had a long-term partner, who began to tug him home again. His visits to Laura became fewer, and when they were together his mobile phone received message after message to which he texted replies surreptitiously. Laura became suspicious, and finally confronted him. Yes, he admitted, there was someone else. She felt utterly betrayed, by her own hopes as much as by him. Worst of all, by her body, which had responded so passionately to his. Suddenly she felt ridiculous. I hope I don't seem self-righteous as I describe the failed romances of these older women. That's not how I feel at all. I envy them. I know I shouldn't, that life is real, life is earnest, and the pursuit of pleasure all too often leads straight to the gutter. I'm old enough to know better. I understand that drugs are addictive so I steer clear of them. Same with too much drink: it turns you into a slurring bore and it's bad for the liver. Gambling bankrupts you, and making too much money taints the soul. The only intoxication I would defend, I've felt it several times in the past and would ecstatically reach for it again if it came my way, is love. Even if it's an ersatz version, fleeting, and based on a daft, self-deceiving infatuation, I say it's worth it. Unless, of course, you have the serious misfortune to end up with a violent criminal, a thief, a murderer or a paedophile, which has happened to all too many vulnerable women. But if you just fall for the wrong person, out of need or desire, and it all goes sour, remember how bright the sunset looked when you watched it together, and how the love song that had sounded so trite before you met him suddenly spoke to you like the most exquisite Shakespearean sonnet.

I'm writing as if this just happens to women but, of course, single men can suffer, if they succumb to a luscious lady at an age when they ought to know better. They, too, end up feeling ridiculous, when the friends and family who had tried to warn them gather round with 'We told you so' bouncing in think-bubbles over their heads. The most famous recent case, I suppose, is that of the world's most eligible bachelor, Sir Paul McCartney. I have met Paul once or twice. I once had a long conversation with his first wife, Linda, and she struck me, as she did everyone, as being genuine, warm and unpretentious. No wonder she and Paul were such successful parents as, heaven knows, not all rich and famous pop stars are. Paul and Linda had a real partnership: they worked together and they played together, because whatever the critics said about Linda's musical skills, they wanted to incorporate each other into everything they cared about. When my husband died, Paul came to his memorial service in St Martin's-in-the-Fields in London, and he said, 'You know, the last time I was here it was for Linda's memorial.' By then he was with Heather.

Looking back, it was a crazy pairing. He was so recently bereaved, she such a mixture of contradictions. The saddest thing about Heather Mills is that she cast herself as a heroine, and she nearly was one. Yet time and again she broke the spell, hurled away her halo, and whirled about like the Wicked Witch of the West, radiating anger. Her website is a rambling, ranting expression of that rage. I saw her close-up when I worked with her and, like so many of her ex-friends, ex-colleagues and ex-lovers, I admired and despaired of her in equal measure. If only, we sigh . . . I was never surprised that Paul, who could have had his pick of the world's most beautiful women, chose her. He obviously loves strong, achieving women, having married one and fathered two more. I first met Heather when she was a guest on my talk show, and I was enormously impressed, as everyone is on their first encounter with her. Just look at the effect she had on American viewers in their version of *Strictly Come Dancing, Dancing with the Stars*. She won every heart. It's not just that she is a sexy blonde, the world has thousands of them. It's not even that she uses her sturdy Geordie accent to such effect. It's the physical courage that drives her on, the way she absolutely refuses to allow her amputated leg to disable her. She dances, throwing herself through the air flamboyantly, she rides, she skis and, given her romantic history, no doubt she is just as acrobatic in bed.

I got to know her best in the half-dozen years we presented a Sunday-morning ITV show together, the series she left in the end to marry Paul. But she was single when, before the series started, we sat together in a photographic studio. She whiled away the time by showing me the jewellery she had hung on to after a love affair broke up. She clearly went along with Zsa Zsa Gabor, who said, 'I never hated a man enough to give him his diamonds back.' Only in Heather's case, I remember, it was a large emerald. I was amused. She was so practical and unembarrassed about her ambition, and as she told me the stories of her deprived and difficult childhood, I understood why the jewellery was such an important prop. Now I know that the stories she told about abduction and abuse actually happened to someone else, not to her, and that doubts have been cast over her tales of hardship, but that just makes the Heather enigma more fascinating, not less. On screen over the years she was an asset to our programme. She worked on some important campaigns, fighting for better artificial limbs to be available for other amputees, and for police to recognise, when they are caught up in a car chase, how dangerous it is when the 'red mist' descends over their eyes, and they drive like demons. (It was a police motorcyclist who cost Heather her leg.) But off screen the anger that is her besetting sin was never far away. When she made mistakes, as we all do, she blamed the nearest technician. Insecurity again: it takes confidence to admit you're wrong, but it made her very unpopular with the crew. As time went by she bitterly resented having to rehearse, and once appeared for the dress rehearsal wearing only a towel, to prove that she'd been interrupted while she was taking a shower. That didn't endear her to them, either. Alongside the anger was the inexplicable fantasy. At that time one of the Sunday newspapers employed a journalist coincidently also called Heather Mills. At a meeting with a senior ITV executive, she convinced him that she was responsible for the other Heather's columns about social services. She came to a ChildLine ball, at my invitation, and told my husband that she had won a dozen BAFTAs. Desmond was on the Council of BAFTA, and he knew that was completely untrue. He came back to me, spitting, 'Don't ever sit me next to that woman again.' Then she was asked to make a film in Cambodia about the victims of land-mines there. The problem was there wasn't a director available to go with her. By chance she happened to meet one of the hottest, most talented producer/directors of the moment, Chris Terrill, who had filmed the BBC's hit series *The Cruise* . . . I'm told that when Heather turns her blue gaze on a man, she's irresistible, he can't escape. Certainly Chris didn't. He agreed to go with her to Cambodia, and under the midnight stars on a boat on the river he proposed and sealed their engagement with a little bamboo ring. She came back wearing it, not quite as chunky as an emerald but just as romantic. Their wedding was bought by *Hello!* magazine, the date was fixed, I was invited and bought myself a ridiculous hat. Heather saved me from having to wear it. A few days before the Cambodia film was broadcast, she went to the Pride of Britain Awards, met Paul McCartney and, in the blink of an eye, the wedding was off.

It's easy to imagine how impressed he was by the tireless campaigner, showcased on the Pride of Britain Awards, enticing in her tight sweater, bravely striding out on her artificial limb, careless of his status as the world's most eligible bachelor. No wonder he thought his beloved Linda had come back again, feistier than ever, to fill his bed. Heather once told me of the electricity between them when they first met, and passion is difficult to gainsay when you are starved, body and soul, of someone who has become half your whole. And Heather adjusted her persona to fit his needs. Suddenly she was vegetarian, although we had filmed her eating chicken curry a few weeks previously. Now she refused, on grounds of animal cruelty, to report a film about a young people's charity fishing event on a lake, so I interviewed them instead. She came into the studio one day wearing a fabulous Stella McCartney suit, with a silk lining imprinted with dozens of lipstick-coloured 'I love you' messages. We knew it was only a matter of time before she blew away on the west wind. And indeed she did, no goodbyes, just Paul waiting in Reception to carry her away.

At this point the story could have gone either way.

Because we all love *Cinderella*, even the most jealous Beatles fan must have hoped that lonely Prince Paul had found the right partner. Although we know fairy tales are not to be relied on, at the time I, too, thought that maybe Heather's dream had come true. At last she could become the person she longed to be, the world-class celebrity, using her fame to benefit the causes she most cared about. And I do believe she cares. I've heard her counselling other amputees, showing by her own example that they can be as adventurous and active as ever. I know of the private acts of kindness she has performed to help her friends. When Desmond died, the first flowers that came to my door were from Heather and Paul. Surely her new security would allow her anger to cool down. The trashy Heather could be laid to rest. If only she had stayed kind, and kept her irresistible blue gaze on Paul, if only . . . Alas, as we know, the marriage has shattered, but as outsiders we'll never know quite why. It's likely that Paul had created a mythical Heather in his mind, which she had aided and abetted by adding gloss and camouflage, but a combination of her anger and the stories that kept emerging from her past eventually demolished their increasingly fragile love.

Characteristically, when she was on her own once more, in spite of the scathing criticism of the judge in the divorce case, Heather exploded on to the world's television screens, raging publicly about the way the media treated her, her fury as raw and unhealed as ever. If we were on speaking terms, I would say to my old colleague, 'Why did you waste your energy? You have a lovely daughter and you will have enough millions to keep you both in emeralds as long as you want. For once, Heather, have the strength of will to dump the Wicked Witch of the West, grab back that halo and become the heroine you so nearly are.' And to Paul I would say, 'There were times with Heather when you were able to forget your grief, and you felt fresh and young again, so if you were seduced into living for the moment, and you blocked your ears to common sense, who can possibly blame you?'

It would be cynical and unfair to assume that all middle-aged love affairs end in shipwrecks. Many marriages that begin with passion evolve into lasting love, and couples gently elide from being Romeo and Juliet to Darby and Joan. As the stress and responsibilities of family life become simpler, and they have more time for each other, husband and wife often develop a new, even deeper partnership: they recognise how similar they have become, and familiarity breeds content. There may still be differences, but even if she takes up bridge and he spends mornings on the golf course, it still leaves them with plenty of time to enjoy the company of friends and relatives together, and explore pleasures they can both share.

Sadly, inevitably, one or other will end up alone. It can feel like leaving a warm fireside and finding yourself, naked and vulnerable, outside in the cold. And some people simply cannot bear that. For them, finding someone, almost anyone, is a physical and emotional priority. But as the stories I've heard and retold already, 'anyone' can be worse than no one. So, how to find the right person, who will fill that unbearable void without replacing it with pain and humiliation? Many people have discovered that the Internet can be a tremendous resource, provided we understand that there are no guarantees. In the virtual world, lies can be told, disguises are easy, and there are unscrupulous swindlers who set out to ruin lives, empty bank accounts and prey on vulnerable targets. So, beware. Then there are the huge, flourishing personal columns in all the newspapers, local and national. Once again, *caveat emptor*, bear in mind that what may be a harmless frolic to one person can be far more emotionally charged and committing to another. If you sincerely want to find a soul-mate, hopefully to be together for the rest of your lives, there are more expensive opportunities, dining clubs where the guests are carefully screened and selected for their compatibility not only in age or background, but also in bank account. And, of course, there are still a few marriage bureaux, even in these unconventional times.

Not long ago I consulted one as a journalistic exercise. I was astonished by the sheer quality of the candidates who had put themselves forward. These were not sad no-hopers. These were attractive, successful people, whose life and work had made it very difficult to meet other single potential partners. There were airline pilots, international businessmen, teachers, medical consultants, salesmen, shop workers, people from every background. They enclosed photographs, another nice surprise. They were a good-looking bunch, some with tattoos, for those who like that sort of thing, some with piercings, many who were clean-cut and, presumably, upstanding. So although I personally didn't find one who would do, maybe I wasn't really in the market, there were many wedding pictures on the wall, sent to the agency by very satisfied clients. It is possible to find another partner, and create a new, lasting relationship, even without technology, or professional help. Take Eve, for example. She had long given up hope when I first met her. It was obvious that she had been a pretty girl, and, as is sometimes the case but not always, in her late sixties she was even more attractive. The blonde of her hair was enhanced with streaks of silver; her colouring had softened but her eyes were as blue as ever. Slim and graceful, she had a natural style, choosing pastel colours and chunky unusual jewellery that looked terrific on her.

She told me that for the last years of her working life she had been the volunteer co-ordinator for a local hospice, and when she'd retired, she'd had time to exploit her artistic talent. She spent a few years happily restoring their dilapidated house with her husband Denis. She was the interior designer, he was the builder and, thanks to their skill and hard work, the shabby Victorian family home had become elegant and desirable. A good thing too, because when Denis unexpectedly suffered a fatal heart-attack at the age of sixty-seven, he left no life insurance and very few savings for her to live on. Eve had no choice but to sell the house they had transformed together. She put the considerable profit into the hands of a reputable financial adviser, and had enough income to go on occasional cruises. She went alone, which was difficult. It wasn't much fun sitting at dinner at a table for one, or fending off the groping hands of male passengers who assumed she must be desperate for company.

On a visit to Lisbon she was strolling by herself down the Rua Augusta, trying to resist the glamorous shoes in the boutique windows, when she saw John sitting at a café table. She knew him from home. He had been married to a friend of hers, but John's work had taken him away and they had lost touch. He asked her to join him and, over coffee, told her he was divorced now from her friend, and he, too, was on holiday by himself, but not enjoying it. They got on well, better than Eve had remembered. They exchanged phone numbers. She wasn't sure she wanted him to ring, but when he did, she was amazed by the way she felt, heart pounding as she tried to keep her voice steady. It was daft, she told herself, to behave like a sixteen-year-old again. They were both cautious, but they knew time wasn't on their side.

Eve told me about the night, six months after they re-met, when John rang and asked her to stay the weekend with him in his cottage in the country. It was a big step for her to say yes. It had been so long since she had made love with someone new, she was frightened that it might be a disaster. She made herself accept. After all, she could always make an excuse and cancel. That evening she looked at herself in the mirror and shuddered. It wasn't a young body any more: there were creases and lines, places where her skin was mottled and where her bones stood out harshly. She turned one way and then another, hoping that the lights in the cottage would not be too bright, and that John would be forgiving. He met her at the station and kissed her on the lips, lightly. Now was the time to run, but she didn't want to.

They hardly spoke as he drove her to the cottage. It was May, and dusk when they arrived. As she walked in she saw he had gone to immense trouble: the table was laid, there were candles on the sills and fresh lilac in the vases. He was just as nervous as she was. She decided directness was the only way. 'Let's skip supper,' she said, and led him upstairs. The casserole was burned to a cinder, but neither of them cared. They ate cheese and ripe peaches, and smiled. From that moment on, they were inseparable.

I asked what made their love work, when many older people find it so difficult to start a new relationship. 'You must remember,' she said, 'that we were friends before. We had a great deal in common. And we didn't rush into it on a tide of passion. And we both had the courage to risk making fools of ourselves. Asking me to go away with him had been a big step for him, too. And I took a gamble when I took him upstairs. The one thing I had to rely on was a very expensive set of lingerie. Thank God it worked.' So what advice can I glean from the couples I've met and interviewed? Only that love can lift your life into a new, dazzling dimension, but even if you fall back to earth with a thump, there are no bones broken. Of course, your pride will suffer but, like a lizard's tail, it will grow again. Try to protect your bank balance. Try to stay in touch with your friends: no matter how envious or disapproving they may be, there's a chance you'll need them again. And if a new love does come your way, and your head and heart tell you it's right, forget the fear, the shyness, the lack of confidence, and seize that moment. It may not come your way again. To paraphrase the quotation I began with, ''Tis better to have loved and been laughed at, than never to have loved, or laughed, at all.'

Chapter Ten

Grandparents

> *Becoming a grandmother is wonderful. One moment you're just a mother. The next moment you're all-wise and prehistoric*

Pam Brown

O dd how God provides compensations. You might think, if your youth was active and fertile, that the loss of sexual allure in old age would be a huge deprivation. Maybe you haven't found it so. Maybe you're still bunny-hopping with as much vigour as ever. Well, lucky you. But in spite of all the passionate couples I met when I was researching my chapter on love and sex, whether we care to admit it or not, the number of people who can, like Mae West, carry on carrying on well into their eighties is comparatively small. As the Gershwins remarked, Methuselah may have lived for nine hundred years, but there's no point in livin' when no gal will give in to no man of nine hundred years. Nor no woman, neither.

So here we are, a little short of nine hundred years, but surveying in the mirror a body that is still perfectly viable, although, as one male friend told me regretfully, he's stiff where he shouldn't be and not stiff where he once was. Goodbye, we say sadly, to the mating games we used to play, and to the proud parenting that followed. Hello, we're grandparents. I'd better admit right away that this is not an experience I have yet enjoyed, but nearly all my contemporaries have, and when I say enjoyed, that's a fantastic understatement. They're delirious with it. One friend has entirely remodelled her house so that she can extend her dining-table far enough to accommodate them all. Her bag and suitcases are bulging with photographs. She beams with delight when she tells you her granddaughter's latest triumph. Another friend rang to tell me, with joy, that her grandson had just learned to open all her kitchen cupboards. I agreed that he was clearly destined for a career in astrophysics. It's important to share the pleasure of a new grandparent if you want to keep her friendship. Do not think for one moment that I scoff at this relationship. It's a vital one, and one that I fear, in these days of being told by politicians to get 'on your bike' to find working opportunities on the other side of the country, or the world, that far too many families are deprived of. I had the great privilege of living in a big extended family. My maternal grandmother, Milly, had four daughters, all of whom lived within ten miles of her home. I saw her once a week throughout my childhood, and my paternal grandmother, Esther, almost as often.

Today that physical closeness is all too rare. We are far more mobile, we have the Internet and jet travel so that we can roam the world, and we do. Marriages come and go, and happen far later in many women's lives. In some ways that offers us far more experiences and adventures than were ever available to previous generations. But there is a cost. As usual, when there's a trade-off, it's the children who suffer. Many of them hardly ever see their grandparents. It's a relationship that's worth holding on to. And it's up to us to do our best to preserve it. Grandparents can provide so much: humour, entertainment, consolation, refuge but, above all, the continuity with our own past that we all need. I have written about 'Winton's children', the Jewish children saved from the holocaust by Sir Nicholas Winton who, just ahead of the Nazi occupation, organised train transport out of Prague for them, and found families to look after them in Britain. Their lives were saved, but most of them lost their families, parents and grandparents, all of whom perished in

Auschwitz. These children lost far more than the physical presence of their parents and grandparents: they lost identity, the certain knowledge of who they were and where they came from.

Nicholas Winton became for many of them their only continuity. In a real sense he became the grandparent their own children could never have, and he revels in the role. He knows the story of their rescue: he was there when the Nazis were beginning their grim occupation of the Sudetenland. He can testify to the heroism of the families who sent their children away alone, on a journey to the edge of the world they knew and beyond. He is the living thread that binds them to their past. They value his company, they are proud of him and grateful to him, and he radiates joy when he is with them. If there is such a role as surrogate grandfather, Sir Nicholas Winton plays it supremely well. In the lucky families where the grandparents are close enough to play a role in daily life, it is, at its best, the pointing between the brickwork, the stuff that holds the home together when harsh winds blow. Of course, the parents are the sturdy walls that, in ideal circumstances, provide shelter for their children, take the weight and carry the load. But every now and then they may grind together, or shift and wobble a bit. Bringing up children is no rest cure, especially when both parents are out at work, or the whole responsibility is carried by a lone parent.

I have met grandmothers who literally saved the lives of

their grandchildren. At the age of seventy-one, an extra-ordinary woman, Sheila, whose daughter had become a heroin addict, took her grandchild to live with her and brought her up successfully. Another, Linda, was alerted when her grand-daughter rang ChildLine to say that she was deeply unhappy in her violent home, and was rebelling by taking drugs and binge-drinking. At the child's request she went to live with her granny and, feeling safe and loved, began to do well in life and at school. Those are extreme examples, but in a thousand more humdrum ways, grandparents can make themselves invaluable as baby-sitters, school-runners, the ones who attend sports day and the school play, sometimes pay off the mortgage and eke out the family income. Often Granny gives the cookery lesson and Grandpa goes to football in a household where, for one reason or another, the parents simply don't have time for these luxuries. Which are not luxuries at all, of course, but necessities for children, knowledge disguised as fun. If I look back on my relationship with my grandmother Milly, 'fun' was the key word. As a toddler I was fascinated by the way she could fashion a mouse from her handkerchief and make it hop up her arm. She sang Victorian music-hall songs, which told stories in a language I could barely understand: 'Last night down our alley came a toff, Nice old geezer with a nasty cough, Sees my missus, takes 'is topper off, In a very gentlemanly way . . .' and the chorus, sung with tremendous vigour, 'Knocked 'em in the Old Kent Road'. And 'Off went the van with my home packed in it, I followed on with my old cock linnet . . .' I didn't have any idea why the home had been packed into a van, I just sang along.

I did ask questions about the life she had led when she was young. I knew that Grandpa was twice her age, thirty-six to her eighteen, when he proposed. And that she'd had a beloved little brother, Peter – his picture hung on her wall and he'd had a halo of golden curls – who had died aged two from diphtheria. Granny had had to learn early about death, as many of her generation did. I experienced it when I was very young. Grandpa died when I was four, and I'm told that when Granny walked weeping around the garden, I ran after her and slipped my hand into hers. From then on we were the closest friends. I remember rummaging through her cupboards and finding treasures from a different age. There were huge books illustrated by Arthur Rackham, and gold-embossed *What Katy Did* and *What Katy Did Next*. There were *A Little Princess*, and *The Secret Garden*, books that centred on clever, brave children, and took me, like a magic carpet, into a world Granny remembered, where girls wore wide sashes, learned improving poetry, and played with hoops. I now own her little silk 'bonsai' tree, which was once covered with glass flowers and fruit, most of which have disappeared now. To other more objective eyes, it must look like a mothy piece of junk instead of the glamorous table centrepiece it once was. Granny had a strange brass lotus that she used as an incense burner, putting the incense into the heart of the lotus, then watching the petals open as it burned. In my childhood such things were never seen in any shops.

Similarly when my own mother became a grandmother she ceremonially bought for me exactly what Milly had bought for her when I was born, a 'royal' pram, glossy and black with a hood and high handles, bouncing on enormous springs. It looked like an illustration from a Victorian children's story, at a time when modern babies were being wheeled around in buggies. But new is not always progress. The old-fashioned pram meant that as you pushed your baby you could talk to him, smile at him, and as he began to fall asleep he could watch the fluffy stuffed duckling swinging from the hood. There is nothing quite as satisfying as tucking your baby snugly into an old-fashioned pram, then clicking the gabardine cover over the blanket to keep out the wind and rain. It's just not the same with a buggy and a plastic hood.

As we become grandparents in our turn, it's part of our duty to educate our young that bread doesn't grow ready-sliced, or peas frozen, and we can remember when they weren't. Maybe we should write down the quaint customs of our past to entertain and educate our grandchildren. The parties of our youth, when we danced the Twist, and the Ladies' Excuse Me. How in our teens 'going out' with someone meant just that, and that before the pill was invented we used to draw the line at 'snogging', or some of us did. Maybe our grandchildren will stare with amazement, and think of us as funny old things. Especially if, like many grandparents, we come from another part of the country, or the world. We may originally have spoken a different language, or observe a different religion, or both. All the better for our grandchildren to learn about diversity at first hand. Even if language and customs have changed radically since our youth, we must learn to communicate with the young. We have so much to offer and, above all, we can give them time. Less pressure means being able to enjoy our leisure time together while Mum or Dad, or both, may be hard at work and exhausted when they get home. Visiting my grandmother Milly was always a tremendous treat. We invariably had meringues for tea; she kept them in a biscuit tin, and they were as unlike the shop-bought monstrosities as they could be. Where shop-bought meringues are white and powdery, Granny's were pale golden, with a crisp, fragile shell and a chewy centre. Pressed together round a heart of whipped cream, they were as near perfection as any food could be. This, in case you have grandchildren to enchant, is the recipe for Granny's meringues, as passed on to her daughter Marion, and thence to her daughter, Jane, to whom I am indebted for passing it to you and me:

4 egg whites, carefully separated so no yolk is present
Pinch of salt
Splash of lemon juice
4 ounces granulated sugar

4 ounces caster sugar
whipped cream

Whip the egg whites with the salt and the lemon juice until very stiff. Add the granulated sugar and continue whipping until stiff again. Then fold in the caster sugar. Place spoonfuls of the mixture on oiled foil or baking parchment, and cook in a very cool oven, (gas mark 1), for about one and a half hours, or overnight in the cool oven of an Aga. Sandwich with whipped cream.

Granny taught me how to make lavender cones. Does anyone do that now? We went together to buy 'baby ribbon', thin satin ribbon in palest pink and blue. We picked lavender from her garden when the flower heads were dry and fragrant, tied them together, then bent the stalks over the flower heads and wove the ribbons in and out of the dry stems until they were completely covered. Then the ribbon was tied tightly again, so that we had created woven satin cones to put into our drawers to perfume our clothes. I have planted lavender in my garden, a magnet for bees and butterflies in the summer. Maybe one day I'll be a grandmother too, and show my granddaughters how to weave baby ribbon through the stems. I learned patience from her, literally: she taught me the card games that have become the basis of 'Solitaire', the computer game. She used to amuse her daughters, my aunts, by cheating when the cards annoyed her by refusing to come out properly. She played Solitaire too, but for her that meant something different, a polished wooden disc with indentations that held dozens of little black balls and one white one. The game was to try and hop the balls over each other, eliminating the hopped-over ball until only one was left, and that one had to be in the middle. Maybe I succeeded once or twice in a lifetime of trying. I'm not sure. We played endless games of Canasta together. Once, after a row with my mother, I went ostentatiously to my bedroom, packed my clothes and wash-kit, and stalked off to school. There, I rang Granny, and said, 'I've run away from home, may I come to stay with you?'

'Of course, darling,' she said, 'We'll have meringues for tea.' Not perhaps the toughest way to discipline a naughty grandchild, but I still remember the stolen evening, my favourite treats to eat, and then a game or two of Canasta. By the time I went home again the next evening, the row had completely evaporated. Grandparents always say the advantage of the relationship is that you can enjoy spending the day with your grandchildren, then give them back in the evening. That welcome separation, the distance created by a gap of two generations, can also be a great advantage to the children. Issues that have become life and death to Mum and Dad are just one of those things to Granny and Grandpa. The wider perspective can allow children to relax and feel safe about confiding difficult, sometimes frightening issues that they may find impossible to tell their parents. That's why it's such a tragedy when a divorce is so bitter that it builds an insuperable barrier between children and their grandparents, just when they need each other most. I've had desperately moving letters from grandmothers whose daughters-in-law have made it impossible for them to see, speak or write to the children they have known and loved since their birth. It's cruel to everyone, and I would beg couples not to allow their own anger to deprive their children of such a valuable relationship.

In Africa they say it takes a village to bring up a child. It certainly helps to have grandparents to support both parents and children. But it can be a difficult tightrope to walk. In-laws don't always get on. So I would suggest a few rules that we grannies and grandpas, potential or actual, would do well to abide by. These are the vices we should, in my view, avoid:

Grabby Granny

One granny I know spread terror among her family: she seized them by the cheeks with fingers like steel pliers, pinching them, then shaking the whole head backwards and forwards as she cooed affectionately. Grandchildren fled when they saw her arriving, nieces and nephews quailed, even if they stood their ground. She did it to my mother once, then a grown adult, when they met at a funeral. Mother and I both saw the granny approaching from the far end of a cloister at the local crematorium. We had plenty of time to discuss how to escape what we knew was coming, but possibilities are limited when you're stuck between large bunches of flowers on one side, and engraved vaults on the other. By the time we'd realised there was no way out, she was upon us or, rather, upon my mother. The fingers were grasping her cheeks and her head was being shaken even more violently than usual, given the emotional trauma of the moment. My mother had pierced ears but, even so, her earrings flew out and were never seen again.

Grumpy Granny

'Isn't it time for that child to go to bed?' 'You're not breast-feeding that child again!' 'That child' is grumpy-granny-speak for 'that appallingly spoiled and indulged child who will turn out to disgrace the family which is why we never spoiled you as a child, and that's the only reason you've turned out OK, or fairly OK'.

I have often been warned not to take a Christmas cruise, because it's full of old men and women who have been wrecking the family Christmas dinner for many years. She (or he, but usually she) has been sitting with her jowls drooping and her lips compressed, complaining that the turkey is cold, that the potatoes are soggy, that the children are noisy, that the pudding is not nearly as good as the one she would have made, had she not kindly devoted herself to her family at Christmas. So, this year the whole family have pooled their available cash to pay to Send A Granny Away (SAGA for short).

My local council once invited me to their Christmas lunch for old people who would otherwise be on their own. It took me five minutes to work out why this tragic fate had befallen a good number of them. They had not a good word to say about anyone, especially about anyone they were related to. So beware of becoming a grumpy granny, or you, too, may end up alone next Christmas, or on a cruise with even grumpier ones.

Greedy Granny

She insists on the first, and best, portion of whatever is going. She wants the icing on the cake. She will take the last sandwich without a blush. She wants her pick of the wine list, even if her son-in-law is paying. The reason is that for many very old people, as with many new babies, the one sensory pleasure they have left is taste. They have been waiting all day for this lunch. Their eyes follow everyone else's fork, jealously, nervous that someone else may have stuck in their thumb and pulled out a plum.

There's only one way to deal with this, if you don't want to become one of the nastier characters from Oliver Twist, bellowing, 'What? You want more?' I recommend that you humour her. It probably matters more to her than it does to you that she gets the slice of cake with the silver balls on it. But greedy granny may find that she gets fewer invitations in the future, if she doesn't mind her manners.

Grudging Granny

It's as well to remember that inflation hits every currency, so the twenty pounds that was generosity beyond bounds when you were young is not such a treasure-trove now. In fact it may only buy one book, just, whereas you could have filled a bag with them when your granny gave you a ten-pound book token. Also, bearing in mind inheritance tax, you may find it worthwhile to give away a little more of your cash, or your jewellery, as you grow older. I wear my grandmother's bracelet with the greatest pleasure, having seen it on her wrist. And the picture that used to hang over her fireplace now hangs over mine, and I think of her whenever I see it, which is every day.

Grubby Granny

That's a real problem. At what stage do you mention to Granny that there is a blob of last week's egg yolk on her cardie, or to Grandpa that there are many varied souvenirs of soup all over his tie? Given that few people's sight improves with time, they probably think it's just part of the pattern or the weave. My mother particularly liked to take her grandchildren out for a Chinese meal. It was a lovely occasion, but we didn't enjoy her favourite starter, fried seaweed, nearly as much as she did. Before long her lips and chin would become encrusted with fragments of curly green leaves, the size and texture, though not, fortunately, with the taste, of pubic hair. Sooner or later one or other of us would give up, lean forward and wipe them off. She took it in good part. How do you avoid embarrassing your own grand-children in this way?

Strong glasses, a bright light, and a flannel soaked in hot water.

Gruesome Granny

Some grannies (and grandpas) don't smell good. They may not notice it, but their grandchildren certainly will. Both my grannies smelled very nice. My grandmother Esther, who always wore a hat with a veil, and played the piano, smelled of talcum powder and lavender. I can smell it now.

Groping Grandpa

You need to be aware of the fact that if he groped you as a little girl, or boy, he may well do the same to your children. Be sensitive to the possibility, and if your children don't want to visit Grandpa, or dread him arriving, ask yourself why. There may be good reason.

Grammarian Granny

' "Isn't", not "ain't".' ' "I don't want any", not "I don't want none".' There are two views about this kind of pedantry: either it's a proper concern for the wondrous legacy of the English language, or it's boring, pusillanimous obfuscation.

Grandiloquent Granny

Two views once again. The granny who holds forth, who writes to the papers, who rings up radio phone-ins, who holds strong views and expresses them forcefully may be a much-prized asset to her community. An outstanding granny my neighbour Peggy Jay certainly was. I recently attended her funeral, which took place on what would have been her ninety-fifth birthday. The church was packed. All seventeen of her grandchildren were present. Her eldest son, Peter, once the British ambassador to Washington and known, poor chap, as the cleverest young man of his generation, gave a glorious eulogy, paying tribute to her bossiness, her vitality and, above all, to her championing of good causes. Whether she was fighting on behalf of children in long-stay hospitals, or against McDonald's changing the quaint character of her high street, she was vociferous and fun. She will be sorely missed, Her local paper called her Queen Peggy, but I can imagine that a granny who lacked her style and charm might be a bit of an embarrassment to her shyer relatives.

If those are Granny's potential vices, there are some equally important virtues for her to cultivate:

Grateful but not grovelling granny

It's crucial that we recognise what a precious gift we receive when our grandchildren are lent to us for an hour, a day, even a week or two. We may be doing their parents a favour by allowing them some time to themselves, but they are doing us a much bigger one.

Gregarious granny

I think all grannies should give loads of parties. They needn't be grand; a few hand-cut cucumber sandwiches and a bottle of ginger ale are fine. But inviting the extended family to join in silly parlour games, as they used to be called (who has a parlour now?) will create memories everyone will savour. My mother's unique style of playing charades is a case in point. Seeing her mime *Free Willy* will live for ever in my memory.

Groovy granny

It's as well to keep up, if you can, with changing attitudes. No need to go too far, to interrupt every sentence with 'like' or 'cool' or 'man'. But being just a little unpredictably mischievous will add sparkle to the relationship. And if we're not constantly shocked by how much and how fast life has changed, we may enable our grandchildren to share their worries and concerns with us.

Gracious granny

And, above all, grannies must be forgiving. If grandson Charlie lets out a rude word, or granddaughter Liza fails to write a thank-you note, forgive them. If daughter-in-law wrinkles her nose at the sausage rolls you've heated up, or son-in-law arrives for lunch late and with his BlackBerry in his hand, forgive them. Be gracious. You are the lifeline that links them with their own DNA. They are your immortality. You need each other.

Chapter Eleven

Politics and Political Correctness

> " *What is conservatism? Is it not the adherence to the old and tried against the new and untried?* "

Abraham Lincoln

Politicians are deeply concerned that fewer and fewer people can be bothered to take part in our democracy. At each election, the vote gets smaller. They think the answer is to woo the young. You and I know that won't make any difference at all. Either we do as they have done in Australia and make voting compulsory or we change our culture radically and woo the elderly instead. Why?

Here's an unfashionable reason. The average child does not become adult until the age of twenty-one. By that I mean the girl child because, to add a sexist gloss, the average boy child does not reach adulthood until he is twenty-five. Only then does the turmoil of glands and hormones calm down enough for ex-teenagers to feel strongly about anything beyond sex, rebellion and their own identity. Frequently nocturnal, addicted to pizza and *The Simpsons*, with a capacity to secrete socks and small change in the tiniest nooks and crannies in the house, adolescents speak their own language and despise the sentiment and sentimentality, which, they believe, afflict their elders. Their churning hormones make them the ideal market for pimple-removing cream, pounding music and radical causes their parents don't approve of.

But the real stuff of politics, the day-to-day issues that go into manifestos, is boring and tendentious stuff to the under-twenties. Politicians, who live in a claustrophobic world of their own where everything to do with politics is feverishly fascinating, are busily lowering the voting age, first to eighteen, and now, they threaten, to sixteen. They believe (how extraordinary is this since so many of them are parents) that having the vote will inspire the currently apathetic teenage generation who don't care about politics and therefore don't listen to politicians, or read what they publish, or vote in any elections.

Speaking as one who, as a teenager, could not have cared less about politics, I see no point in fighting nature. The boys I knew who were active politically did it for hormonal reasons, because 'there were girls in CND' or 'I left copies of *Spare Rib* around and it worked brilliantly.' The girls did it because a cause like 'Ban the Bomb' was simple and straightforward enough to put on a banner, and would infuriate the stuffy old-fashioned previous generation. If I'm insulting your principles, if you were a child of the sixties who was genuinely politically active and have stayed that way all your life, I apologise. But you must know that you are in the minority. Far more young people vote for *Pop Idol* or *The X-Factor* than would ever dream of voting in local or national elections, and I would have been one of those young people.

But not any more. Now I wouldn't dream of wasting a phone call on Will Young or Leona Lewis, much as I admire their talent and enjoy the shows that found them. However, I feel utterly committed to voting in any election that affects my life, local, national, for the London mayor, any of them. What's more, I have become a news junkie, feeling deprived and out of touch if I spend too many hours without watching or hearing a news bulletin. Prime Minister's Questions holds me riveted. I remember my parents being concerned to read newspapers and catch every bulletin; the nine o'clock news on the Home Service was a nightly ritual, but as I grew up I was mystified. All this tedious stuff about foreign affairs and the economy, what kept them so spellbound? I know now.

So, I suggest that politicians focus their attention on the people who are listening to them with close attention: the over-forties, obviously not to the exclusion of the rest of the population, but remembering that we are their heartland. We are the generation who will actually get out of our homes on rainy nights to go to the polling booths, or who have taken the trouble to fill in the forms to obtain our postal votes. We care.

Mr or Ms Pollster, you probably believe that we middle-aged fogeys are a lost cause because we made up our minds decades ago. If so, you are quite wrong. Some of us perhaps did, but many of us are persuadable. That's why Margaret Thatcher won. It's also why Tony Blair won. We, who listen and care, are the holders of the middle ground, and both those consummate politicians knew how to appeal to us. But the overwhelming temptation for everyone who works in market research, it seems, is to try and pursue the notoriously fickle, self-absorbed teenagers, and in the process ignore or underestimate us. It's crazy, when the 'elderly' (nasty word) are set to become the largest section of the population. In sheer numbers we are significant.

Remember, pollsters, when you read the latest survey saying that older voters are unreachable by argument, that this is not the first time you have come to the wrong conclusion. I'm sorry that I always laugh so heartily when the pollsters' predictions are utterly overturned by results, but it is very satisfying. We knew it all along. Their problem is that it's their professional religion to have faith in the results of the surveys they make their money conducting. I've taken part in some of those surveys, and I can tell you that the whole process is quite different from voting. So, politicians, stop listening to the youth-obsessed pundits: listen to us. Another quick apology. I constantly meet well-informed, articulate young people who take part in organisations like the Youth Parliament. No doubt they include the parliamentarians of the future, maybe I've already met the next prime minister but ten. However, they must admit that they are not typical of their generation. It's not that I underrate people of their age, it's that I fear the pollsters and the politicians overestimate their capacity to woo and win the young vote. So, what is the quickest way to our hearts, we baby-boomers who are determined to vote, but haven't yet determined who we will vote for? (Or for whom we will vote, if you prefer: I, too, can be a grammarian granny). That depends. We come in two major categories. With time, we have become either mellow or extreme.

Let's take the mellow fellows first. When I attended Prime Minister's Questions for the first time, having long been fascinated by it on television, I watched Tony Blair facing what has to be one of the toughest gladiatorial contests in the world, but my eyes were drawn to an eighty-year-old Member of Parliament sitting on one of the green leather benches near the back. He was a huge man, imposing and charismatic, a star, and he obviously knew it. For years he had been in pride of place in my personal gallery of baddies, the Reverend Ian Paisley, with his unconventional doctorate, plus the fire and damnation sermons he gave in which Catholics were inevitably the demons. But that was then. A few weeks after my visit to Parliament, Dr Paisley and his arch-enemy Gerry Adams were photographed in Belfast not just power-sharing but roaring with laughter at the same joke. So many lives lost on both sides, so many unforgivable things said, and yet these two sworn enemies had recognised what we all know in our hearts, but so often forget: that peace is better than war, and there is far more that unites us as a species than divides us. What had brought about this extraordinary change? There were, of course, many factors in that most complicated country, like demographical changes, and the water rates (odd but true), but most of all I think it demonstrated the triumph of experience over hope. The Reverend Dr Paisley had experience of the misery that hate and anger bring. The hope he had as a young man, that he could extinguish all opposition, was clearly never going to be fulfilled. Compromise was the way ahead, for him, for his nation, and for the future. And if we learn anything as we grow older (and some people don't), it is that the future no longer belongs to us so it's our duty to protect the next generations. Otherwise they will rightly blame us for the mess they inherit from us.

Inherit. There's a trigger word. We over-forties are, it is said, obsessed with the unfairness of inheritance tax. After all, the argument goes, we have already paid ample tax on the money we leave, why should we be re-taxed when we die? But each small concession by the Chancellor sets up a chorus of protest from vocal campaigners, who accuse us of being selfish and greedy. No, we're not. The only people who, I can guarantee, will not profit if inheritance tax is abolished (not that such a thing is likely) are us. By definition, by the time the tax is imposed we won't feel a thing. We'll be past worrying. So in resisting this tax while we're alive we're being totally altruistic: we want to be able to give away more of whatever pot of gold remains after our death to those we leave behind. And that's another aspect of our thinking the politicians don't seem to understand. They assume that all we older people care about is our own welfare, that we will vote with our pockets. So they talk to us about pensions, and personal care, and our other financial anxieties. Well, yes, we do want to hang on to our financial independence as long as possible. But we care even more about education, and safe streets, and the protection of children and animals from cruelty, and freedom from crime. We put our money where those campaigns are. All the major charities who work in these fields depend on the 'grey pound', donations from their older supporters. Not much selfishness or greed in that.

The other accusation by those who denigrate us is that we

are ultra-conservative, that we hate and fear change, and pathetically hang on to the traditions of our youth well beyond their sell-by date. However life changes, the calumny goes, we will defend the status quo until barnacles hang on our bums. To take one example: education. (Here, because it touches a nerve, I'm going to give way to personal polemic. Do skip the next few paragraphs if (a) you think only comprehensive schools have any right to exist, or (b) all separate special-needs schools should be abolished. If you, like me, think that the baby has been thrown out with the bath water all too often, keep on reading.) It is claimed that we who are 'too old to change' cling to the English public schools because they preserve the class system, and we are much more comfortable if we all know our place, the rich man in his castle, the poor man at his gate. Piffle. Have they forgotten that we were children (or in my case in my twenties) in the sixties? We threw out the fifties subservience. We reinvented satire and irreverence. We aren't motivated by a rigid refusal to accept new ideas, far from it: our DNA contains revolution and radicalism. But we were born in the shadow of the Second World War, and we lived through the Cold War and Vietnam. So the truth is that we oldies are fed up with any kind of war, religious, ethnic or class. The reason we will protect the best schools in the land against attack, be they public, grammar, comprehensive or faith, is not because we want to preserve barriers or create wars. It's because the traditions we hang on to, the ones we were brought up with, whatever our income and our background, include a love of British culture, good clear handwriting and a ready acquaintance with the multiplication tables. And maybe a little Latin and Greek to boot. Sadly, you are likely to find more of that in the public schools than in some of our failing comprehensives. But if someone suggested (and I wish they would) that half of the places in our major public schools should be reserved for scholarships for academic children from poorer backgrounds, we would march in the streets of Eton to campaign for it.

I was educated at a 'direct grant' school, operating on that very principle, now obliterated. What a loss. My class at school was completely diverse in terms of income, and we neither knew nor cared what anyone's father did for a living. Someone may have been the daughter of a publisher, someone else's father was a builder's labourer. What we had in common was that we were motivated to learn. Grammar schools had the same levelling effect: pupils were selected for academic excellence, rather than their parents' income. But, of course, not all children, or adults, want an academic education. That is another 'politically incorrect' thought, because, when it comes to learning, we are peculiarly snobbish as a nation, particularly the hard left. We think it's an insult to suggest that some young people might gain a sense of direction and achievement if they learned a trade, rather than struggling with a Shakespeare sonnet. Other countries are quite happy to create vocational qualifications for young people who want to gain a skill, and they prove their worth – look how fantastic Polish plumbers and painters are. In my consumer-champion days, I devoted many programmes to that other great British tradition, the cowboy workman: he didn't care a jot how much muck and mess he created, and his one ambition was to squeeze as much cash out of his poor client as possible. If he's feeling the pinch now, good. But I'd far rather he was being elbowed out by newly trained, enthusiastic, hard-working Brits, than by excellent craftsmen from Poland. It's up to our educational system to give our young people the opportunity they have in Poland to gain those skills. But enough. Much as I have enjoyed taking up your time and attention with opinions I've gathered over a lifetime, and which I think of as the middle ground (and even if you don't agree with the ones I've picked I'm sure you have bushels of opinions that you, too, have preserved over the years and would enjoy sharing), it's time to leave these tranquil meadows and clamber up the rocky steeps of extremism.

It's wonderful how some granity old politicians keep their radical views utterly uneroded by the winds of change, like Tony Benn, for instance. Once, to his horror, destined for the House of Lords, he discarded his double-barrelled name and peerage and became one of the most admired speakers in the House of Commons. Having left it, he is still constantly in demand. It's a wonder to witness his brilliant mind roaming around the world's conundrums, analysing the cause of every problem, casting blame, as he clothes his arguments in a mixture of wit, compassion and mischief that challenges and entertains his audiences. And I do mean audiences, because well into his eighties he can fill theatres with people of every age, there to admire the firework display of his diatribes. What a man! Not that I want him anywhere near real power or decision-making. That would be catastrophic. One of Benn's favourite topics is that politics should be based upon issues, rather than personalities. I've never followed his drift. Is he saying that the personalities of Hitler and Stalin were not relevant to their leadership, that it was simply a matter of the deeds they committed, rather than the men they were? I've always thought the opposite. Reading a manifesto is one thing, but trying to guess how far a new leader will stick to the rules once he has the levers of government in his hands, how honest he is, how power will change him, whether he is charismatic enough to take the country with him, and if so, where he will take it, those are some of the most important calculations we voters must try to make.

My father always said he would rather vote for an honest fool than a clever rogue. It would be nice to have a less bleak choice. But all too often Fate gives us horrible surprises. Britain notoriously misjudged Idi Amin, and failed to predict what a monster he would become once he had the power to kill and persecute anyone he wished. Amin was not unique. If only the people of Zimbabwe had been able to predict the madness of Mugabe: how much misery would that beautiful, formerly prosperous country have been spared? If only the people of Germany had understood the full horror of Hitler's immense capacity for evil. If only Stalin's brutality, and Mao's sadistic insanity had been probed by isometric tests and revealed to their constituents. Those are the lessons that we, who have watched the world wag for forty or fifty years, have learned. Isn't it a paradox that Benn himself, whose personality is so engaging, should have tried to persuade us that in politics it's irrelevant?

Malcolm Muggeridge was another example of a grand old extremist, in his eighties as far out on the right as Benn is to the left. Muggeridge, once editor of the humorous magazine *Punch*, had made the traditional journey from left to right: starting as a womanising socialist, he ended as a Puritanical Catholic, a typical paradox. Claiming to despise the medium, he loved appearing in television discussions, where his face took on the expression of a man sucking an especially sour lemon as he sneered at the excrescences of the modern world, its obsessions with sex and materialism. He was witty and articulate, and intellectually arrogant, refusing to accept any other argument or see a different point of view. He, like Benn, became a national treasure. You, too, may be one, as entrenched in your political views as Muggeridge or Benn. But wherever you come in the spectrum, there are a couple of political phenomena today that I am prepared to guess irritate you as much as they do me. One is the party political broadcast. These are designed to put anyone off politicians.

For one thing they are intolerably boring. There was a time when Margaret Thatcher, foolishly, decided to remove the voices from television of Northern Ireland's Sinn Féin politicians. I was asked to give evidence to some parliamentarians at that time as to whether losing the 'oxygen of publicity' would prevent bombs and other acts of terrorism. I offered the reverse solution. Force them to make party political broadcasts every night, I suggested, first because, as Churchill said, 'Jaw, jaw is better than war, war', and second because they are deeply unlikely to gather support: party political broadcasts are not only dull, they are completely unconvincing. 'An election is coming,' said T. S. Eliot. 'Universal peace is declared and the foxes have a sincere interest in prolonging the lives of the poultry.' The trouble with politicians who are trying to persuade us to vote for them is that motive is written so clearly in their eyes that it's impossible to take them seriously. I really don't know why they spend so much money on their campaigns when basically what we want to know is, can we trust them? Are they bright enough to sort out the inevitable crises that will leap out of the darkness and threaten us all, be it global warming, blue-tongue disease, MRSA, or the new plagues nobody has thought about yet? And finally, but less importantly, are they clean and tidy enough to make a good impression and secure the best deals for us when they go off on a jaunt round the world?

The second, even more irritating, syndrome is the

misapplication of political theory transmuted into 'political correctness'. Back in the eighties, on *That's Life!*, we created the concept of a 'jobsworth' award. (And if you doubt our authorship, you have only to consult the *Oxford English Dictionary*. We brought the term to the British public, who adopted it and now cannot remember how they ever did without it.) A 'jobsworth', of course, is someone who is stubbornly determined to apply a rule, regardless of its inappropriateness. The car clamper who disables the car belonging to a dad who has paused in a hospital car park to rush his wife into the labour ward before she deposits their new baby on the asphalt: that clamper got our jobsworth award. Political correctness belongs in the same mould, the slavish creation of a rule within the general concept of a benign principle, which has the opposite effect. Take child protection. Oh, my Lord, it's a jungle of political correctness. We know that paedophiles will go to any length to get into close contact with children so it's important to be aware of the potential danger. But that is absolutely no excuse for preventing proud grandparents videoing their granddaughter playing the Star of Bethlehem in the school nativity play. Yet some officious local education authorities create and apply that stupid ban. Sports coaches sometimes abuse their students: notorious cases in Olympic teams have hit the headlines. But that's no reason why a pool attendant should not be allowed to jump in if he suspects that one of the children is nervous of the water. Come on, local councils, you cannot be serious! But, alas, they are. I remember being extremely timid when approaching the local Santa in his grotto in a big London store: above his cotton-wool beard his nose was red and bulbous, and he smelled nasty when I sat on his lap. It all happened in public, in front of a long queue of similarly diffident children. Is that good enough reason to check all Santas for criminal convictions?

In one of my guises I occasionally meet children who are being looked after by their local authorities. One of them, I'll call him James, told me he'd rung ChildLine in the past. My nightmare is that a child who needs help rings ChildLine but can't get through. So I asked whether James had managed to speak to one of our counsellors, and if so, whether it was helpful. He said, 'Yes. I was being bullied, but they gave me some advice, and now the bullies are my best friends.'

I was overwhelmed with delight. 'James,' I said, 'that is such fabulous news I'm going to have to give you a kiss,' and I lightly kissed the top of his hair. He and I are still in touch, I'm happy to say, and he's doing really well. But a day or so later the CEO of the charity came to tell me she had received a complaint about my inappropriate behaviour. Thou shalt not kiss a child, even on the top of his head, even if he feels validated by the fact he knows I care about him. AAAAAAAAGH. How many teachers who have cuddled a child when she has fallen over, and been reprimanded for it, feel as I do? In whose interest is this insanity? Certainly not the child's. Are we really to treat children as if they are inanimate objects, with no emotions or emotional needs?

Then there's the minefield around disability. Recently I noticed a screen-saver bearing thoughts about 'Deafness or Disability'. Having been deaf myself, I asked why the distinction? I was told by a (hearing) person that deafness is not a disability but a 'different ability'. Now, the problem with that concept is that if deafness is not a problem, it doesn't need a solution. I am a patron of a charming charity called 'Hearing Dogs for Deaf People', which does just what it says on the tin. They rescue unwanted dogs, train them, give them to deaf people, and the dogs transform their lives. Deafness can be a very isolating condition: newly deaf people sometimes become so depressed at the loss of communication that they stay imprisoned in their homes. But give them a cheerful little dog who needs exercise, and who wears a jacket identifying it as a 'hearing dog', and suddenly people want to pat the dog, talk to you, and understand that when they start a conversation they must face you. That's in addition to the fact that the dog can alert you if the doorbell rings, or the telephone, or the alarm clock, or the smoke alarm.

But if deafness is not a disability, just a different ability, there is no need for a hearing dog. Nor should anyone have a cochlear implant, because that interferes with deafness. Never mind that it also allows deaf people independence, and gives them a form of hearing that, although not exact, transforms their lives. AAAAAAGH. And that in turn leads to the debate about special-needs education. There are those who will tell you there is no need for the 'ghettoisation' of special education for disabled children, that education should be 'inclusive', and all children educated together. Alas, this has become the received opinion, so I was lobbied by desperate parents trying to save a wonderful school that had developed unique skills in communicating with, and educating, deaf-blind children. Just imagine the isolation of those children's lives. We failed, it had to close. Heaven knows where those remarkable teachers went: the double disability is so rare that no school that did not specialise could afford to employ them. I have received a number of tragic letters from the parents of deaf children who were so badly bullied in mainstream education that they not only didn't want to go to school, they didn't want to live. I met these suicidal children, and they told me that school was a daily torment, being kicked downstairs, and beaten up on their way home. But there exists a school, the Mary Hare School, which was created for bright deaf children. I visited them, and because of their (politically incorrect) emphasis on teaching their pupils to speak and lip-read, their sixth-formers were impressively articulate, so much so that in many cases their deafness was undetectable. What's more, in that community they felt entirely 'normal': their teachers knew automatically, for instance, that they must not speak with their faces turned to the board and away from the class.

The school had resident technicians who could repair hearing-aids whenever they broke.

I managed to obtain scholarships at Mary Hare for the bullied children I met, and they stayed in touch with me, reporting their achievements with joy. Hooray! Self-esteem restored. Disability to a great extent overcome. The headmaster explained to me some of the obstacles placed in his pupils' path. When they applied for university places, instead of recognising how much more difficult it is for a deaf student, and therefore relaxing some of their entrance requirements, many universities actually insist on yet higher grades. And why not, if deafness is just a 'different ability'? I just pray that Mary Hare survives this crazy era of 'political correctness' in which deaf children are not supposed to learn to speak, just to sign. The headmaster explained the problem there, too. Sign language is far less rich in synonyms: if you want your students to have a full, varied vocabulary, they need spoken, written English. But who dares point that out to the militants? Another charity with which I am involved sent out an official memo about 'diversity'. In it I was told that since the term 'political correctness' is 'invariably' used to undermine diversity strategies, it should be prohibited from use. I sent a memo back saying it was, in my view, politically incorrect to ban the phrase 'politically incorrect'. AAAAAAAAGH.

Could it be that what we oldies have is common sense? And that we watch the madness of the world and shout from time to time, 'Do you realise the Emperor has no clothes?' And isn't it time that the world paid attention? It will, but only if we are prepared to enter politics ourselves. There's the rub. In our ageist times the much-vaunted virtue is youth. But what we need in Parliament, in local government, everywhere that political decisions are made, is candidates with life-experience and common sense. Us. It's not enough to follow the news and vote when required. We have to stand for election ourselves. It won't be an easy ride. Menzies Campbell, recently the leader of the Lib-Dem Party, was heaved out on the ground that he was too old. He became the butt of gibes and cartoons, but in reality his age was not the problem. He wasn't too old, he was too boring. John McCain was not too old to win the Republican nomination. Nelson Mandela was not too old to lead South Africa. Ronald Reagan was not too old . . . Well, maybe he was. But we are not, you and I.

So maybe we should stop enjoying ourselves, stop making the most of the chance to travel, learn ballroom dancing and have all the fun I've tempted us with in previous chapters so that we can serve our country and our community. Get political. Not for ourselves, but as a matter of duty, honour and responsibility, which are, after all, the principles we have learned to value more than selfish pleasure. Aren't they?

Chapter Twelve

Tradition

> *The novelties of one generation are only the resuscitated fashions of the generation before last*

George Bernard Shaw

It was Sunday morning in Rarotonga, the capital of the Cook Islands, and the white limestone church was packed. The Pacific Ocean there is so warm and lush that oysters produce huge, lustrous pearls, and the reef swirls with brilliant fish. Outside the hot little church the hibiscus was in scarlet bloom and the lagoon was shining with stripes of deep blue next to aqua next to silver, watered silk over the satin of white sand.

Nobody in the congregation was tempted to plunge into the ocean. They were there to worship, and they did so in style. In spite of the heat, the men were in suits, the women were in pastel cotton jackets, no unseemly flesh showing, and neatly trimmed cream straw hats woven out of coconut palm. The electronic organ played the introduction to the next hymn and they burst into song, in an explosion of sound, the deep male voices producing syncopation like a Maori war dance, the women holding their hands in the air, part in entreaty, part in exultation. I've never heard singing like it. It put the faltering choirs of English village churches to shame. A few days earlier, Dorice, the local chief, had taken me to the *marae*, the sacred ground where her clan had held her investiture. A fine-looking, elegant woman, she was also a hotel-owner with impeccable taste, and she took her duties as clan chief extremely seriously. Before we set foot on the *marae*, she and Papatua, my guide, had picked some palms and stripped the fleshy green leaves to make a ceremonial garland. We stepped together on to the wide circle of grass, and she explained to me the significance of the stones strewn over the ground.

Because the missionaries had been draconian in their desire to destroy the existing religious rituals in the Cook Islands, the special investiture throne of solid rock had been destroyed. They had had to find another in the heart of the jagged volcanic mountains that frame every view in Rarotonga. It was immense, and heavy, and the fork-lift truck operator had been terrified of blaspheming the hallowed ground of the *marae*, so he had dumped it just outside and fled. Dorice told me that the priest had started to chant, and she and a few muscular warriors had attempted to lift the stone. By some miracle it had been light as a palm leaf. So she was properly invested, including the moment when she had to bite the right ear of a decapitated pig, to symbolise that she would always listen to the concerns of her people. That, too, must have been a fascinating ritual to behold.

The missionaries never quite stamped out the old ways, I'm happy to report, although they did their best, or worst. I know it's wrong of me, but on Fiji when I noticed in one museum case the scorched leather soles of a pair of boots, that being the only part of a missionary the villagers had been unable to eat, something in me was pleased that there had been at least one moment of cultural revenge. But those days are long gone, there have been ceremonies of truth and reconciliation since, in which the descendants of the eaters have shaken hands with those of the eaten, an interesting mixture of DNA, though it's probably not true that you are who you eat. Now the Cook Islanders are particularly good at supporting two widely different cultures side by side. Church and *marae* are equally significant, both enriched by the spirituality and fervour of the population. I have no doubt that rituals and traditional ceremonies fulfil an instinctive need, and that we baby-boomers have a special responsibility to keep them alive, and pass them on to the next generation. Even on a micro-level, rituals are important in our family lives, creating landmarks that are engraved in our memories. There is no question that some of the most moving events of my life have been religious ceremonies or secular rituals. Family birthdays, my second wedding (to the same man), my husband's memorial service, my parents' funerals, my children's bar and bat mitzvahs, Princess Diana's funeral, Christmas in Salisbury Cathedral or in my cottage barn, all were made memorable and inspiring by music, poetry and the people who shared them. Like the Cook Islanders, my family are ecumenical: we celebrate Jewish, Christian and pagan festivals with equal enthusiasm.

Faith is a deeply personal matter. It has been the cause of wars, acts of indescribable cruelty or outstanding self-sacrifice. It can unite or divide like no other issue, so I don't intend in this chapter to venture beyond the shallows. But it also contributes lustre to our everyday lives, like those iridescent Cook Island pearls on a fisherman's string necklace. We owe it to the next generation to give them the chance either to preserve or reject our personal traditions. Maybe they'll dump them with relief. Certainly that seems to be the way many religions are going at the moment. But perhaps they won't. I admit I'm delighted that my children still insist upon their 'birthday tables' and their Christmas stockings, and so do I, even though they are in their late twenties and I'm well over sixty-five.

Each birthday entails special preparations either the night before or at dawn. We arrange the unopened cards and gift-wrapped presents around a central birthday cake, splendid in its silver or gold frill, an inscription in pink or blue icing, and the candles ready to be lit as the birthday girl or boy approaches. 'Make a wish,' we shout, as they slice the cake and, for some reason lost in pagan tradition, we shriek as the knife hits the plate – is it to let out the devil?

On one terrible morning the devil answered back. My elder daughter Emily leaned forward to blow out her candles and her hair caught fire. I froze with horror, but thank heavens my husband didn't: he leaped at her and smothered the flames. It's surprising that birthday parties haven't been banned by Health and Safety, at least in our household. Christmas stockings are often really pillow-cases, to encompass Father Christmas's liking for large teddy bears and such. The problem was always that he deputed to us parents the chore of placing the stockings at the foot of each bed, and it was an uphill struggle for us to stay awake later than our children. One year Desi could stand it no longer. Our eyelids had stuck together at least three times, our heads fallen forward on to our chests, and we just couldn't fend sleep off any longer. So he tiptoed upstairs and was hugely relieved to find the children sweetly asleep. Each stocking was placed on the end of a bed. Then, just as he was tiptoeing back to Emily's bedroom door, she sat bolt upright and shouted, 'Boo!' She says he jumped two feet in the air, and only then did she remember his heart condition. Family rituals in our home often had that edge of danger. On his sixtieth birthday Desi decided not to celebrate. Old age, he felt, had overtaken him and there was nothing left to look forward to, still less to pop the champagne for. I didn't agree at all, so I decided he would be forced to celebrate, whether he wanted to or not. I told him we'd go out for a birthday supper for a lugubrious Chinese meal with my mother. MSG invariably gave him a headache, so did my mother, so it was sadistic of me, but I was cross with him. How could he try to deprive us of celebrating such an important milestone with the man who filled our lives with joy? Secretly I invited all his favourite people, some of whom he hadn't seen for many years so they were thrilled by the idea, and told them to be in place in our sitting room by six o'clock. He and I spent an exhausting but happy day together at the Chelsea Flower Show (a great advantage of a surprise party is that you have to delegate all the last-minute preparations), then returned to a dark, quiet house. As Desi opened the door to the sitting room, all the lights went on, crackers exploded, and sixty voices shouted, 'Surprise!' The video shows Desi's face turning a pale grey. Once again I realised, too late, that I had risked killing him with a heart-attack. But of course he adored the celebration, and spent a very happy evening reminiscing with those special friends.

It takes time and experience to create a memorable event. My first wedding, though a joyful occasion, was a bit of a shambles. As we had put it together in three weeks, details like a carefully orchestrated table plan went out of the window. (We had, *force majeure*, to offer our guests a buffet, which does have one great advantage. Your guests aren't stuck for what feels like a lifetime sitting next to people they wouldn't voluntarily share a lift with. That happened at one friend's wedding, and I had to leave before the pudding. Boredom at our age, though rare, is unbearable. After all, when you have limited time left, spending it with people whose conversation makes you writhe with tedium is not to be tolerated.) Also, as I was eight months pregnant by the time my wedding day arrived, standing for hours in towering high heels was an ordeal. The register-office ceremony was infiltrated by a London evening paper, whose reporter went round our family and guests asking, 'What do you think of Esther being pregnant at her wedding?' We left the reception and drove for a weekend's honeymoon, all the time we could afford to take off, in a trendy hotel by the Thames with a Viennese chef. He insisted on serving us an Austrian wedding breakfast. We knew that Sigmund Freud had been Viennese, so the symbolism, as course followed course, made us giggle helplessly. First there were cones of bright pink smoked salmon stuffed with cream cheese. Then there was an immense pink sausage flanked with two wrinkled pouches made of cabbage stuffed with rice. Finally there was a towering skyscraper of orange ice-cream, decorated with globs of whipped cream. When at last we were alone, bridegroom turned lovingly to bride and said, 'Come here, barrel-belly.' The next morning the waiter brought in our breakfast, asked me for my autograph, and then, when I proudly signed it Esther Wilcox, made me do it again. The second wedding, nearly thirty years later, was very different. Desi had by then converted to Judaism. (I said to him, ungraciously, 'And to think I went to all that trouble to marry out.' But, of course, I was thrilled, and suggested to him that we could celebrate with a synagogue ceremony.) He had already suffered two serious heart-attacks, and I was determined to make a public commitment of my love for him. With great care I crafted a service that would incorporate his favourite pieces of music. We booked a Klesmer band (the wonderful *Fiddler on the Roof* combination of wild violin and clarinet), and as a special surprise a soprano to sing his favourite song, 'May to September'.

The rabbi, David Goldberg, whose sermon was crammed with many excellent jokes at our expense, was as surprised as I was that, as I walked down the aisle to the wedding canopy, I was almost fainting. How could that be when, in the eyes of the law, I had been married to Desi for so many years, and had three children by him? Fortunately the rabbi had Rescue Remedy hidden in his robes, which he kept handy in case fragile brides needed it, not that he had expected me to go fragile on him. But emotion moves us in unexpected ways, and I still remember the sight of Desi, the man I loved and had lived with for nearly forty years, all dressed up in a beautiful grey morning suit, waiting to take my arm. And so the prescribed rituals unfolded. The vows, the sharing of a cup of wine, the exchange of rings (both, alas, now on my fingers, and there for life), the breaking of a symbolic glass (why? It's a mystery lost in time, but it provokes the congregation to turn to the nearest single person and wish them, in another mysterious translation from the Yiddish, 'Please God by you'), and then the reception. This time our son Joshua, also resplendent in grey, made the best man's speech (more jokes at his parents' expense). Then we drove to our cottage in the New Forest, to enjoy the late-evening sunshine. I had promised Desi that I would cook our supper this time, and I did. We shared two tins of Beluga caviar, and I prepared the hot toast, butter, hard-boiled egg yolk, finely chopped onion, and a little sour cream. With champagne to wash it down, what could be a more delicious picnic?

The great value of these rituals is that they have immeasurably enriched my memory store. Suppose we hadn't had that ceremony? Desi died so soon afterwards, and it's a wonderful comfort to me that he knew how much I cared for him, and how many of our friends and family wanted to share that extraordinary day with us. So here is my advice, if you, like me, have the privilege of living with your soul-mate. Things that really matter are rarely said, as couples ricochet between the tough targets they set themselves. Compel yourselves to take a day and set it aside, fill it with the sights, sounds and family traditions that mean most to you both. Renew your vows, or create new ones. Collect your favourite pieces of music, the songs of your youth, the ones with special significance. Give each other gifts: they may be precious materially, or only have spiritual value. Create a memory book of the day, filled with pictures and thoughts from those you invite to share it. Parties are our responsibility, now that we are the age of (young) matriarchs and patriarchs: they help us keep our family members in touch with each other. Not that I expect us all to be on speaking terms – what self-respecting family is? There is another great Yiddish word, 'broigus'. It means the smouldering disgruntlement, the grudge that grows from a tiny slight, perceived or actual, into mammoth dimensions. One of my first cousins married without inviting me to the wedding. His sister, recognising the broigus this created not only in me but in all my fellow first cousins, invited us to an un-wedding party, at which I sang a version of 'The Day We Went to Bangor', which included the line 'Massive marquee, no room for me . . .' It was greeted with enthusiastic applause by all my fellow-broigusees. I'm not sure we've forgiven the bride and groom yet. So it's best to make sure when you decide to give a family party that you invite the whole family tree, trunk, branches, twigs, the lot.

Some baby-boomers have taken over the format of This Is Your Life for special landmark parties. It's worth leaving out the embarrassing moment when the star, or victim, is told, 'You haven't heard this voice for thirty years,' and is then called upon to try and identify it. That never went well in the professional televised version, and it certainly doesn't when you fail to recognise your mother's voice. But it is fun to fly over a son or daughter from the other side of the country or the world, and people go to great lengths to keep the secret right up to the moment of revelation.

We created many and varied surprise parties in my family, my husband being the perfect victim, because he was so much more efficient and organised than I was that it never occurred to him I could actually stage-manage such a complex set of arrangements. If you, too, have a very efficient spouse, I recommend you surprise them but, as previously discussed, if there's a possibility of a heart-attack, go easy on the surprise element. Which brings us to funerals and memorial services. They can go badly wrong. I had a cousin who was a psychiatrist. Born a Jew, he became a Buddhist. He was greatly loved, and when he died, far too young, the crematorium was packed. The clergyman who took the service was the chaplain to the psychiatric hospital where my cousin worked, and decided to conduct a very high-church Anglican service. This did not please either the Jews or the Buddhists in the congregation. Furthermore, he kept referring to my cousin as a physiotherapist. This certainly did not please the many listening psychiatrists, who began to growl with anger. That wasn't a sound I'd ever heard at a funeral before, but I can definitely bear witness to the healing power of rage: we were all far too distracted by feeling furious to break down in tears.

Those who attended Hughie Green's funeral, as friends of mine did, also found it memorable for the wrong reasons. On arriving at the crematorium they were surprised to see a large ITN satellite dish. Hughie was the nation's most famous presenter of talent contests, his being *Opportunity Knocks*, but that had been some years before his death, so the newsworthiness of his funeral was not obvious. Hughie's catchphrase had been 'I mean it, most sincerely', but judging by events at the ceremony, sincerity may not have been Hughie's greatest strength. The 'eulogy' was given by his self-styled oldest friend, a tabloid journalist, Noel Botham. Botham used the moment to drop his bombshell. He told the startled mourners Hughie had revealed to him that a very famous female television personality was in fact his love-child. It was unusual material for a funeral oration, but it explained the presence of the satellite dish. In a very short time, helped along by 'clues' from Botham, the tabloids had identified Paula Yates (the ex-wife of Bob Geldof, whom she left for Michael Hutchence) as the love-child. Until that moment she had always assumed her father was Jess Yates, another rather extraordinary British television personality known as 'The Bishop' who, in spite of his own unconventional sex life, had created a career for himself as a slightly grotesque organ-playing host of a religious programme, *Stars on Sunday*. Paula was deeply upset by the sudden allegation, had a blood test to try to disprove what Botham had said, but to her horror her DNA matched Hughie's. The moral of this sad story is that if secrets are to be revealed beyond the grave, the funeral might not be the most tasteful place to do it.

I had the privilege of attending Princess Diana's funeral. No one who was in Westminster Abbey that day will ever forget it. All too often the crowds thronging the streets outside the Abbey weeping as they watched her coffin pass by are described as 'hysterical'. In my experience they were nothing of the kind. I spoke to as many of that crowd as I could, to try and understand why they were there. Some had brought their children. One family I met, a group of homeless people, had come from Glasgow and spent the night on the pavement to make sure of a good position. They felt a genuine sense of loss, and I believe they were right. Nobody else in public life had displayed such empathy, such intuitive warmth, for the most vulnerable people in our society. She cared, and they knew it. I saw close-up the way she communicated with abused children, talking to them about their pain: I was impressed and moved by her sensitivity. She really did understand, and knew how to unlock their feelings. She was generous, too: I remember she walked into a room at ChildLine where a couple of young people were waiting to meet her. At once she spotted the camera they had optimistically left lying on the table, though they would never have dared ask permission to use it. She saved them the trouble by saying, 'Does anyone want a picture?' It wasn't etiquette, but it provided them with a photograph to treasure all their lives. When her life was snuffed out, no wonder the crowds mourned: the dispossessed were her constituency.

Inside the Abbey there was a mixture of the famous and the unknown, stars, aristocracy, her staff and members of her charities. The music was equally an eclectic mixture of ancient and modern, classical and pop. Elton John sang new words to 'Candle in the Wind', renamed 'Goodbye England's Rose', and it felt entirely appropriate as Diana's coffin was covered with white roses, with a card from Prince Harry addressed to 'Mummy'. Then her brother Charles Spencer spoke. He could have been safe, discreet, conventional. He was nothing of the kind. He spoke for all the people in the Abbey and in the crowd who felt they had been robbed. He excoriated the paparazzi who had hunted her to her death. At the end of his speech, the crowds in the streets and parks began to applaud. The sound was like a huge wave roaring through the walls of the Abbey, so that we, the members of the charities she had helped so much, joined the applause. It rolled up the aisles to where the great and the good, royalty and nobility were sitting, and they had no choice but to join in. It felt as if someone had at last spoken for us in an expression of our rage that she had been totally consumed by the heat of our passion to see more of her, hear more about her and, above all, take pictures of each second of her short life. I can't pretend it was a cathartic service, but afterwards, as I walked with some of her colleagues to Kensington Palace, to look at the ever-growing mountain of flowers, it was a healing time, quiet and reflective. The people there, mourning together, were like any family surveying the flowers after a funeral, and realising how much she would be missed. As indeed she is, still.

Was that the funeral Diana herself would have wished, controversial, public, divisive, but moving and memorable? Ten years later, her sons put together a memorial service, and she would certainly have been proud of that, of their courage, and of the way they spoke about her, as a princess and as a mother. Most of us will never have the second chance of a memorial service. Even though a funeral is for the people we leave behind, for their sake we *must* ensure that they know exactly what kind of funeral we want. It's the most important gift we can leave them.

Since we live in an age where a video camera is available in every store, and on almost every mobile phone, why not leave them a message? I interviewed a charming, intelligent, terminally ill man for a programme I made called *How to Have a Good Death* and asked him what message he would like to leave for all those he cared for. He told them to love one another, and love life, and he put it so beautifully that when he did die, they watched his message over and over again. It was such a source of strength and comfort to them that I commend the idea to you. At our suggestion, he talked in detail about his funeral with his wife. He had not intended to as, he said, he had left it to her. But once again, because we persuaded him, she was able to put together a service filled with his favourite words, read by members of his family. That was another tremendous source of comfort for them. So take a moment today: jot down the prose, poetry or music that you would like put together for your friends, colleagues and family to remember you by. Trust me, it will be your most precious legacy to them.

Sometimes it's as important to break with tradition as it is to preserve it. You may find that the holiday you have always taken, the way you always celebrate Easter or your birthday needs a vigorous shake and a reappraisal. That's fine. None of us wants a life filled with compulsive obsessions, always eating the same breakfast, brushing our teeth in the same way, eating the same Sunday lunch. We need to keep freshness in our lives, because every now and then we can discover an improvement. Marmite may be a welcome change from marmalade: we won't know until we try.

Also, it's worth occasionally trying someone else's ritual. I find that wandering into a great religious building, even though it's not my religion, like Salisbury Cathedral at Christmas time, is a glorious experience. It's as if the prayers of centuries are hanging in the music-filled shadows, the hopes and fears of all the years, and in that moment I become part of a universal longing for peace, and love, and refuge.

This is very personal territory, and your views will be different from mine. But we have it in common, we who have experienced a good deal in our time, that we owe it to the next generations to have the same amount of choice we had ourselves.

Remember the missionaries on Cook Island, who would have cut away and destroyed the rich traditions of the Maori culture they found when they landed. They were wrong. Remember the old ways, and with luck and tolerance they will comfortably coexist with the new, and then, like a hymn in a Rarotonga church, a wonderful harmony may be created. Thanks to you.

Chapter Thirteen

They Don't Write Songs Like That Anymore

> *The longer I live the more I see that I am never wrong about anything, and that all the pains I have so humbly taken to verify my notions have only wasted my time*
>
> George Bernard Shaw

One of the sadnesses of growing older is that we have had to live through the day the music died. By which I do not mean the death of President Kennedy, or any of the other elaborate decoding of 'American Pie', wonderful song though that it is. I mean that for all of us there were the glorious songs of our youth, followed by a great chasm that was filled with the roaring, crashes and bangs, the cacophony of today. I'm not sure when you would place the tragic day when they stopped writing songs like they used to, but I *am* sure we all recall our first experience of great music.

For me it was when my father reverentially carried the family gramophone (a state-of-the-art piece of technology in the 1940s), a heavy box with a green lid and wind-up handle in its side, to the centre of the dining-table. Then a black shiny record (produced by HMV, I know, because it had a picture of a dog on the label listening devotedly to His Master's Voice) would be taken out of its sleeve, and the playing head of the gramophone unclipped from its safety catch. Very gently my father would place its great head, balanced on a tiny, sharp needle which had to be regularly replaced because it wore out very quickly, onto the outer groove of the gramophone record. As it swung slowly towards the centre there would then be a swishing, crackly noise, and eventually we'd hear a soprano carefully enunciating her way through 'Ring a Ring o' Roses, a pocket full of posies . . .' and we sang along. To me there is a satisfying continuity about the fact that children have been singing nursery rhymes for centuries. The 'ring' in the song originally referred to the rosy red rash which was a symptom of the bubonic plague. More than three hundred years later, to me and my chubby toddler friends it just meant the chance to fall over and roll around giggling.

Isn't it fun that in 'Pop Goes the Weasel' the 'weasel' was actually a 'whistle', short for 'whistle and flute' (Cockney rhyming slang for 'suit')? So that song was really about taking your suit to a pawn shop, not the story of an exploding ferret. And isn't it sad that these nursery rhymes have gone out of style, and no longer echo around playgrounds or primary schools?

Alongside the nursery rhymes I sang in my childhood, I loved and learned specially written children's songs like 'The Teddy Bears' Picnic.' They, too, have long gone out of style, but the great news is that if like me you haven't heard those songs of our childhood for nearly seventy years you can hear it again on YouTube. Ah, the miracle of technology that can bridge the years, so that suddenly you're a toddler again, hopping around to that other masterpiece, also recorded by Henry Hall, 'Hush, Hush, Hush, Here Comes The Bogey Man'. Which, I suppose, was the 1940s version of a horror movie. Those masterpieces were written in the days when songs were written especially for children, and they were considerably more ambitious than the stuff my own children learned at nursery school: 'The wheels on the bus go round and round, round and round, round and round, the wheels on the bus, etc., etc., etc.' I sang about Nellie the Elephant who said goodbye to the circus, and the sad story of the shoemaker, who made some special shoes for the lovely girl who made his heart go pop, and asked for shoes to set her feet a-dancing, but when he made them, just whirled out of his shop without a backward glance. See? Real preparation there for life's inevitable disappointments.

There was even a programme on the wireless on Saturday mornings specifically for children's favourites, when they would play 'The Ugly Duckling' sung by Danny Kaye, and my grandfather's clock, which ticked and tocked for ninety years, but then stopped short never to go again when the old man died. I used to think I was the only person to remember the songs of my youth. Then one afternoon when I was appearing in 'Dictionary Corner' on *Countdown* I started to sing 'A, You're Adorable' and suddenly the whole audience was joining in, through B, C, D all the way to Z. Not just catchy, improving. But the astonishing thing was that everyone in the studio remembered it too, music and words for a song that was last a hit in 1949. And it wasn't just memory we had in common: the reason we were all in that studio together was that we loved language and brain-teasers and, although I didn't test this hypothesis, we spent some of the day listening to Radios Two and Four on the BBC and the Magic and Classic independent stations. On those stations they offer quality in speech and music, and we baby-boomers have learned to tell the difference between quality and trash. After all, we've lasted pretty well ourselves, and seen the trash come, go, and get chucked away, a few bits and pieces to be recycled, but a heck of a lot sent into oblivion.

However, I am aware that I am, once again, straying on to dangerous ground. Of course it's a matter of taste. What I think of as quality you may despise as trash. Take Nina Simone. She lifts my heart, and restores my soul. But you may say, 'Maria Callas, yes, she is true quality, but Nina sings trivial rubbish.' (As Nina was herself trained as a classical pianist I suspect she would agree with you, but to me, the precision and musicality of her singing and playing demonstrates just as much artistry as Ms Callas, whom I also adore.)

So let's just test our memories and see how much we have in common. For example, did you live through the fifties, as I did, in a state of mild exasperation, at least when it came to popular music? (And did you know the top ten wasn't even invented until 1952?) Hit songs seemed to oscillate wildly between the cheerfully daft, 'If I Knew You Were Comin' I'd've Baked A Cake', '(How Much Is) That Doggie In The Window', and the glutinously sentimental, 'Unforgettable', 'Secret Love'. I'm not knocking these works of popular art, I merely point out that compared with Rodgers and Hart, or Jerome Kern they do lack a little something. And, of course, the fifties also begat Elvis. But apart from him, most songs were so unsatisfying it was tempting to rely on the richness of the past, the classics by Cole Porter, Irving Berlin and the Gershwins. ''S Wonderful', 'Blue Moon', 'I Get A Kick Out Of You', 'Night And Day', 'Our Love Is Here To Stay', 'Smoke Gets In Your Eyes', and 'Love For Sale'. Even now when life gets tough the sound of Ella Fitzgerald singing any of those is enough to get me on my feet again, humming. The amazing craftsmanship of those songs, the effortless rhymes, the haunting melodies – those songwriters were giants of their time and any time. Furthermore they could turn the clichés of love into something fresh and telling, ''S wonderful, 's marvellous, you should care for me.'

It was indeed awful nice to have people like the Gershwins around to put young love into words and music. So we put up with the trite fifties, feeling in our hearts that something better would come along. And it did. Maybe it's not fair that we who lived through the glorious sixties should make comparisons. How can anyone compare with, for instance, Lennon and McCartney? They can't. Except, of course, George Harrison. How does it happen that three and a half songwriters (much as I love Ringo, we can't pretend he's in the same musical class) should meet, write, perform and outclass anything that was happening around them? The sheer poetry of 'Eleanor Rigby', the vision of 'Imagine' (released in 1971, so maybe it's cheating to allow the sixties to claim it, and Yoko's influence is much more obvious than Paul's, but we can't leave it out), the exhilaration of 'She Loves You', the poignancy of 'Yesterday' – make your own list: every composition shines with brilliance. And there were so many others around at roughly that time: Burt Bacharach, Ray Davies and the Kinks, Randy Newman (every time I hear 'Simon Smith And The Amazing Dancing Bear' I have to stop whatever I'm doing, wherever I am, and listen), songs that had ambition and freshness. Pity those who came before and never heard them. Pity us, whose taste was moulded by them. Pity still more deeply those who came later, and profess to admire punk. Now, please. I fully understand why the genius of the songwriters of the sixties may have given the subsequent generation an inferiority complex. But to try to compensate by elevating the spewings of untalented adolescents, who simply wanted to vandalise any concept of musicianship or literacy, is nonsense. Also, not kind to them. With their frantic posturing and unclean habits, they clearly needed help, and all they got was cynical exploitation by people who should have known better. I once went to an event called the Tin Pan Alley Ball, quaint name. It was to honour the pop stars of the moment, and many of them were there. It was striking that the stars were young, and ill-looking, and everyone else was fat and middle-aged, clearly making a fortune out of the thin, pale singers who had made the hits of the moment, but then would be tossed aside and replaced. There was no feeling of talent nurtured or protected. And certainly no thought of creating careers that would last longer than a few months, if that. At this point let me remind you of the true and alarming history of Georges Bizet. He was incredibly talented, a musical prodigy like Mozart, playing and composing music in his cradle, and winning the top prizes as a student in Paris. When he was in his thirties, he wrote *Carmen*. Can you imagine a more exciting, dramatic, riveting musical experience than that opera, among the most performed and the most enjoyed around the world? Wouldn't you have loved to be in that first-night audience on 3 March 1875?

Well, if you had been there, chances are you would have been growling with indignation, tut-tutting, and maybe even walking out. That first-night audience loathed everything about *Carmen*. The critics called the libretto 'obscene'. They said the music was 'undistinguished, colourless and unromantic'. Bizet had two heart-attacks and died two months later, on 3 June, at the age of thirty-seven. And that just serves us right, we the Philistine masses. If we had been more sensitive, more open-minded, had had better taste, who knows? Bizet might well have given us more masterpieces like *Carmen*. As it was, we broke his heart. So while I'm excoriating punk music, there is a bit of my brain that tells me, 'Watch it, Rantzen, you could be completely wrong, punk could be the *Carmen* of future generations, and Johnny Rotten our Bizet.'

But I doubt that. And, given my loathing of punk and my lurking fear that it, or something like it, might re-emerge, as a parent I regarded it my duty to educate the young, who might otherwise get confused and never find their way to listening to the music we grew up with. So I've made sure that my children are all familiar with the Beatles' opus, and the best of the rest. And while I recognise that there have been songwriters since the sixties – Abba, for instance, infectiously catchy – for me nothing they wrote quite rivals 'Fool On The Hill', or 'Lucy In The Sky With Diamonds'.

Nobody writes songs like those any more. In our own time we have lived through a version of the *Carmen* débâcle. The world-wide phenomenon that is the musical *Les Misérables*, based on Victor Hugo's saga, was greeted with howls of dislike and derision by the critics when it was first performed in England. Fortunately, producer Cameron Mackintosh managed to sort it out and keep it going long enough for word of mouth to prove the critics badly wrong. In the end it became Britain's longest-lasting musical.

Why did those original critics hate it so much? I suppose because it dared to tell a tragic story and nobody was used to musicals that did that. Also it was French, not American or British. Or . . . don't ask me. Now that we are familiar with Claude-Michel Schönberg's magical score and Herbie Kretzmer's clever words, the whole thing is so moving and evocative that it's impossible to understand why everyone didn't notice that when it opened (although I gather it did go on for a day and a half in its original version). I have taken my family to it several times, over the years. Most memorably, it was my daughter Rebecca's birthday treat when she was about seven. It reduced her to tears, of course, but not just a discreet little drop or two rolling down her apple cheeks. Becca doesn't do discreet. She was howling with deep, savage sorrow. Her eyes were crimson, her face was swollen and blotchy, and she continued to give out wrenching sobs as she walked with me down the stairs and out of the theatre. I had just launched ChildLine. I glanced shiftily around to make sure there were no paparazzi witnessing what looked like a wicked case of child abuse: 'Esther Rantzen, chair of ChildLine, today reduced her own daughter to sobbing anguish . . .', you know the style.

Musical theatre has a particular place in my heart, and judging by the way it has taken over theatres round the world, I am not alone. I suppose like many of our generation I began by watching pantomime. You may scoff, but I expect many a fan began by singing along to the song sheet with Buttons or Dick Whittington. Then my parents got more ambitious and took me to Humperdinck's *Hansel and Gretel*. I was five at the time and, unlike Mozart and Bizet, was not a musical prodigy. I'm told I applauded the orchestra tuning up, and thought then it was time to go home. When I was ten, my parents took me to Rodgers and Hammerstein's *The King and I* in New York, with Gertrude Lawrence as Anna and Yul Brynner as the King. I was hooked. The extraordinary score, combined with the exotic setting and a strong story line, held me spellbound. Not least because Yul Brynner was the sexiest, most charismatic performer I had ever seen, and I recognised that at the age of ten. (Just as Marlene Dietrich noticed it at far closer quarters in her middle years. Her daughter tells the story that when she was an old lady, still performing but held together by a dress reinforced with a pink rubber corset, Marlene suddenly straightened up and lost twenty years. Then her daughter saw Brynner sitting in the front row. You must never disillusion a lover, if you can help it.) Anyway, in New York's production, Yul Brynner was fabulous, but I couldn't understand why they had cast that old lady who couldn't sing as Anna. Gertrude Lawrence, bless her, was letting herself down. There's a lesson in that for all divas who carry on too long, and shatter their own legends. My father saw Pavlova dance at much the same stage in her career, and he never forgot the sad parody of her glory. I have had a particular admiration for Oscar Hammerstein's lyrics ever since I saw (seven times) the film version of his masterpiece, *Carmen Jones*. I wonder whether there's a jinx on that wonderful opera? Dorothy Dandridge, who played Carmen Jones quite brilliantly, insolently alluring, irresistible (as director Otto Preminger found), so clearly deserved an Oscar. Yet she was passed over, perhaps because she was black (Grace Kelly won that year, 1955, for *To Catch a Thief*).

So our taste in musical theatre was shaped by the Americans. And still, if you want to see dancing and singing at its extraordinary best, Broadway is unbeatable. But we Brits, too, have made our mark, first with Lionel Bart, our version of Irving Berlin, who never learned to read music but had a remarkable gift for melody. Lionel arrived at just the right moment to take the wicked irreverence of the time and make it sing in 'Fings Ain't Wot They Used T' Be'. It was the theme song of the social revolution that the sixties created, and anyone who saw that original production of *Oliver!* will have been enchanted, as we all were, by a glittering little Cockney blonde, Barbara Windsor. What a star, then and now. Until then the accent of the British musical had been clipped and beautifully enunciated, like Noël and Gertie. But then Bart wrote *Oliver!*, set in the London that he, as an East Ender, knew so well, and in it he revealed himself as a writer with the most extraordinary range, from the boisterous 'Food Glorious Food' to the yearning and passion of 'As Long As He Needs Me'.

And then along came Andrew Lloyd Webber. Let me state my position here bluntly. He has his detractors, but I've always thought, If it's so easy to be Lloyd Webber, why hasn't anyone else managed it? Like the chara-loads who fill his theatres, I am a fan. I adore *Joseph and the Amazing Technicolor Dream Coat, Cats, Evita, Phantom of the Opera* and *Jesus Christ Superstar*. Furthermore, I am a fan of *Grease*. As long as there are am-dram companies in the world these works will live. There has been a bit of a dry period recently, with musical theatre depending on compiling existing works by Queen and such, which, commercial as they are, lack the true spark for me.

What point am I making? That we, the baby-boomers, love the theatre, and we never come late. And many of us have money to spend on our leisure (and to go to the theatre these days, especially the musical theatre, you certainly need a well-loaded wallet). Many surveys have proved that we are the heart of theatregoers, so give us more of what we want, please. It's worthwhile paying attention to us, because without us, you, O Impresario, would be hard-pushed to find an audience. Look what happened to cinemas pre-Spielberg. During a very unpleasant period in the early seventies violence reigned, with 'artistic' products like Peckinpah's *Straw Dogs*, and audiences dropped. There was enough violence in the streets, and in the world, without us paying good money to leave our comfortable sitting rooms, go out in the wind and rain, and pay good money to watch it being simulated. We voted with our feet and cinemas in the seventies were uncomfortable, grubby and empty. Then along came Steven with *Jaws* in 1975, on which he was cutting his teeth, so to speak, and the classic *ET* in 1982, and entertainment was back. Audiences were provoked into crying (I still cry every time I see *ET*), and laughing and taking our children, and being utterly absorbed by a great story-teller, the way the early Hollywood moguls, monsters as they undoubtedly were, intended. Look at wonderful classics, like *Star Wars*, and all the Indiana Jones sagas, and rom-coms like *Sleepless in Seattle*. Yippee, they're terrific, and we walk out at the end of a cathartic evening with an additional spring in our step, thinking the world is a great place after all. Not quite the Peckinpah message.

There was a mysterious moment in the Oscars ceremony in 2006 when *Brokeback Mountain*, the shoo-in favourite, didn't win. Everyone had predicted it would. It was brave. It was ground-breaking. It dared to say that a cowboy could be gay. But for all the hype and hullabaloo, a far less trumpeted film, *Crash*, was actually awarded the Oscar for best film. Why? Well, we who don't belong to the esoteric world of the expert film-buff but do enjoy the cinema can explain. As a voting member of the British Academy, I sat watching *Brokeback Mountain* until the first scene of explicit sex, then turned to my daughter and asked, 'Are we enjoying this?' We weren't. Not because we are homophobic but because we weren't enjoying it. So we took our encrypted DVD out of the machine, and watched something else. *Crash*, which also has its explicit moments, was so brilliantly scripted, directed, plotted, performed and put together that we were carried along from beginning to end. It's about story-telling, you see.

Just as when we listen to popular music we like the lyric to be well crafted, and the music to be tuneful, when it comes to the cinema we like a tale well told. It doesn't have to be simplistic. Remember, we were admirers of Ingmar Bergman and the Nouvelle Vague when we were young, so we like allusive, poetic movies. But we also love the glamour and excitement of James Bond in nearly all his guises, and Michael Caine and Harrison Ford. The story doesn't always have to end happily: we enjoyed *Cat on a Hot Tin Roof* and we loved *Gone With the Wind*. It really helps to make us laugh, as Jack Lemmon and Walter Matthau did in *The Sunshine Boys*, or Mel Brooks and his team in *The Producers* and *Blazing Saddles*. And it's almost unprecedentedly fabulous when a director takes a classic from our youth, like *The Lord of the Rings*, and makes a masterpiece. Like many of us I first read

Tolkien when I was a student (in fact, one of my lecturers was his son). I was enchanted by the Old English atmosphere of Middle Earth, the strange new languages Tolkien had invented, the maps and folklore, the magic of the whole creation. When I heard it was being converted to a cinema blockbuster my spirits dropped. How could Peter Jackson's possibly live up to the scenery and characters version I'd imagined as I'd been reading the book? By some mystic alchemy, against the odds he did it. His Oscars were entirely merited: his achievement was to win over all the Tolkien fans, and make new ones for the books.

The same is true of some of the Jane Austen film adaptations, once again risking the fury of those of us who have been fans of her work most of our lives. That's the other peculiarity of our age group: we read. Joanna Trollope is our muse, and Patricia Cornwell. And, best of all, Alan Bennett. We love their care, their craft, their sharpness. Once again, it's sheer quality. Everything I've said so far about the way musicians, composers and authors can please you and me and therefore make a decent living is naturally based on my personal preferences and prejudices, but at least I have some evidence that you may share some of them. Commercial success is a measure of our support. But one art form completely flummoxes me. Do you admire Damien Hirst and Tracey Emin? Would you spend millions on a dissected cow or an unmade bed? Can you explain this phenomenon? Recently I was trying to attend a Chagall sale, thinking it might be possible that I could afford one of his enchanting fantasies, at least as a print. When I arrived at the auction house in London, I was surprised by the rest of the clientele. They seemed to be wearing ripped clothes, so at first I felt concerned for them. However, as I looked more closely I realised they were very expensively ripped clothes, with raggedy hems, and jackets with fleece spilling out, 'distressed', in fact.

Then the sale started, with a good many bids coming over a line of telephones staffed by a row of shiny, well-groomed young people. But not a Chagall in sight. Men in aprons kept bringing out big blank canvases with the occasional diagonal rip across them, or tiny doodled noughts and crosses in pencil. I soon noticed a pattern. If there was any obvious connection between the title of the work of art and what had been scrawled on the canvas, it would probably go for a mere fifteen or twenty thousand pounds. If there was no connection at all, it would doubtless sell for three or four hundred thousand. I had to fight a powerful urge to leap to my feet as all this was going on and shout, 'Stop! You've been conned! This is a load of garbage!' But, of course, I didn't. The entire industry depends on everyone being taken in. Otherwise all their precious 'investments' would suddenly be worth nothing. Bring down the house of cards and they would turn upon you and tear you limb from limb, distress you more severely than their own jackets. I decided not to risk it, and slunk out.

I know only too well that I am open to the accusation that yesterday's rebel is today's fuddy-duddy. No doubt you are, too. We have lived through exciting times when the rule-books were torn up, not least in television. I was, as I have said, trained in the sixties. Ken Loach was making *Cathy Come Home*, the film that caused so much shock that it led directly to the campaigning work of the brand-new homeless charity Shelter. *Z Cars*, an edgy police series, was transmitting live. *Dad's Army* was gently making fun of the Home Guard, as would never have been allowed twenty years earlier.

Where I worked in current affairs we, too, were breaking new ground, by offending people on purpose, and even more effectively by accident, with late-night 'satire'. I remember our programme was almost taken off the air one week when our designer, as an afterthought, in a sketch with a vicar, made a pipe rack for him that looked like a crucifix. We walked very tall, we saw ourselves as bringing gusts of fresh air into the musty old establishment.

We were constantly frustrated and infuriated by the censorship imposed by our bosses. The BBC even had a rule-book containing the words and phrases that were totally forbidden to us, including jokes like 'That's enough to make a Maltese cross.' We agreed that it should be banned on the grounds of lack of humour, but couldn't grasp why it was thought so offensive.

While I was a researcher on a satire show produced by Ned Sherrin, creator of *That Was The Week That Was*, and then in

1966 working on his last TV series, *BBC 3*, Ken Tynan, the iconic theatre critic, uttered the first F-word on television. Ned, always urbane even when it took every muscle to maintain the image, turned to us in the control gallery and asked loftily, 'Is that some kind of a record?' It was, and furthermore, as they say, it opened the floodgates. So you could say it's our fault that comedy has almost drowned in a tide of F-words. We certainly wouldn't want the old censorship back – far better to label programmes clearly so that viewers can avoid what they choose not to hear. However, one unlooked-for result of relaxing the rules has been that comedy writers and performers too often rely on four-letter words in every punch-line to provoke a laugh. It's lazy, and it has shouldered out other more lasting kinds of humour. And yet shows like *Dad's Army* and *Fawlty Towers*, performers like Arthur Lowe, Ronnie Barker, John Cleese and David Jason have a God-given gift of investing their characters with warmth, rather than simply being caricatures. The humour arises out of relationships we recognise; the scrapes the characters get into are almost believable, and the lines we all remember, the 'Don't tell him, Pike' are rooted in those characters. It's not that writers have forgotten how to produce that kind of enduring comedy: in America, with *Friends* and *Frasier* they're still doing it. But the US has one great advantage over us: Americans are far more Puritanical than the easy-going British, so they are denied the easy way out of using a shocking word to tag a joke. Instead they have to do something cleverer, and funnier. Genius, of course, can break every rule. Billy Connolly, Rowan Atkinson in *Blackadder*, Ricky Gervais, anything written by Richard Curtis transcend the generations.

But the point of this chapter is that if you want to make money out of us baby-boomers, and many of us have money to spend, please don't insult us with crap. Oh dear, there I go, another four-letter word.

Chapter Fourteen

A House Is Not a Home

" *The palace is not safe when the cottage is not happy* "

Benjamin Disraeli

A house has become more than just our shelter from the stormy blast. It's our hedge against inflation, our entertainment on television, our source of curiosity about the rich, and disgust when we see how badly some people live. There are programmes and publications, a whole industry telling us how to make-over our property, how to invest in more property, how to design and build the ideal new house, how to restore and renovate the old one. But in all this highly priced advice and guidance, one aspect of a house has been neglected. A house is not itself a home. And all of us need a home. No matter how nomadic or chaotic or non-materialistic we are, we need somewhere comfy to come back to at the end of the day. Even if it's only the same old park bench, next to the same old rubbish bin. We need a home. Over the years, if you're like me, our needs have expanded. At first we only needed a womb, then a cradle, then a cot, then a bed. As a child, we may have shared a room; if we were lucky, as we got a little older, we may have had a room of our own. We grew up a little more, and had a room in a college. Probably fairly Spartan, maybe very untidy and grubby. There's something about the young human that likes disorder, stuff all over the floor, drawers open, bits of this and that flung around. Then we progressed, perhaps, to something a bit smarter, maybe a bit tidier. And suddenly we felt the urge to build a nest: we wanted a flat, a house, a place to call our own. Still later, if we were even luckier, we found someone we wanted to share our place with. And maybe kids came along, who also needed living space. And all this time the place we lived in had grown and grown.

At what stage in our lives do we start to mind what our homes look like? After all, they were only originally designed to keep out the wind and rain. As long as a cave was waterproof, and primitive man could put down a carpet of leaves, he had no complaints, although the occasional pre-historic handprint or dancing gazelle may have been the signature of a particularly house-proud hunter-gatherer. Medieval halls look magnificent today with their black beams and vaulted ceilings, but imagine them filled with smoke and stench, and suddenly they're not quite so enticing. And in any case they were not exactly cosy: they were obviously designed to impress the peasants with the owner's status, rather than provide a warm, embracing shelter. Even castles had their downside, the moats must have been fairly disgusting pools of rubbish and ordure, when you see that the latrines were poised directly over them. But somewhere along the line, whether it was a Roman emperor's villa, or a Tudor statesman's palace on the river, appearance began to matter, even more than function. Those houses were a visible statement of success.

There was another downside to their magnificence. Stately homes, like Blenheim or Woburn Abbey, are so grand it's difficult to imagine lolling about in your pyjamas, eating baked beans on toast. And although it may be difficult to summon up sympathy for the original owners, they created glorious destinations for our tourist industry at considerable cost to themselves. The Marlboroughs went bankrupt trying to finance Vanbrugh's gorgeous ideas for Blenheim. It didn't get any easier, as the years went by, to pay for its upkeep. Consuelo Vanderbilt Balsan wrote a fascinating autobiography, *The Glitter and the Gold*, describing what it was like to be a hugely rich American heiress forced by her ambitious mother to marry the then Duke of Marlborough who obtained the equivalent of seventy-five million dollars' worth of railway stock as dowry in order to pay for repairs to the roof. In spite of Consuelo's beauty, and her warm heart, it was a loveless marriage, and she left it, the duke and the gorgeous stately home with some relief.

Woburn is just as intimidating, all gold-encrusted architraves and dining rooms built to house the Canalettos. A stately home is rarely a real home. I remember a Duchess of Bedford looking in despair at her echoing halls, and telling me how she longed for the little house she used to live in, before her husband came into the dukedom. Today's generations are grateful to dukes through the ages for creating and preserving such magnificence, now that we are allowed to hire a few of those marble halls for our humble weddings. But would we have wanted to take on all that cleaning, polishing and shoring-up ourselves? I guess for most of us the answer would be no. But in our own ways, and on a smaller scale perhaps, most of us also like to embellish and gild our living spaces to impress our friends and, even more, our enemies. We want their eyes to pop with admiration, and their hearts to shrivel with envy. And that's in spite of the fact that getting all the work done in our own living space can be extremely worrying, costly and uncomfortable. So it's irrational, this instinct to expand and decorate our living spaces at the expense of our own comfort.

When I say expense, I mean it. I have a friend who bought a large house in the country. It had a perfectly serviceable short drive leading to the nearest stretch of road. I was amazed when my friend decided instead to create a two-and-a-half-mile paved road through trees to his door so that all visitors could admire his estate. Even more than the car, the 'hise' (to rhyme with 'mice', the upper-class term for the building people live in) is for some people a crucial status symbol. If you've got it, and want to flaunt it, gold bath taps and a two-mile drive are *de rigueur*. I had an aunt who went further than most in that direction, Great-great-aunt Amy. She married Uncle Arthur, a reasonably successful stockbroker, who bought a grand mansion for her, called Bessemer House, in South London. Amy and Arthur, according to family legend, went on a cruise in the mid-nineteenth century, and on the ship Amy met a charming interior designer. She hired him, and together they splurged on Bessemer House. She took pictures of the result, the grandest room being the huge hall, lined with mahogany, with bear and tiger skins on their chins scattered over the dark wood floor. Fortunately in her time the species were not yet endangered. The resulting bills bankrupted poor Arthur, who dropped dead on his way to renew his life insurance, which was found in his top pocket. Alas, it, too, had also just expired. She was quite a woman, my great-great-aunt. As a newly bereaved widow, she went to visit an old friend and said to him, 'Well, Otto, you always wanted to marry me, and now you can.' So Uncle Otto did. For years I searched for the remnants of Bessemer House. I knew it was somewhere in Denmark Hill, but I could never find it. Then I took a friend to King's College Hospital, and drove into a car park along a road called Bessemer Way. I looked more carefully at the glass and steel hospital buildings I had often visited before, and for the first time I noticed that they were clustered around a central Victorian structure with a flight of stone steps. Suddenly I remembered a photograph of Amy and Arthur posing there together, he two steps higher than she, to make up for the discrepancy in their heights. I parked the car and walked into the main reception. There were the usual glass partitions, signs, noticeboards and lino everywhere, but with a little imagination I could see where Amy's mahogany galleries had once been, and the tiger skins. So yesterday's status symbol is today's hospital, a very worthwhile piece of recycling.

Other mansions have become schools, or hotels like Cliveden, or tourist attractions. Most have to work for their living one way or another, these days, even Buckingham Palace. And I'm not sure I'd choose to live in any of them. That's the advantage for us baby-boomers, living past the age of envy. We no longer feel competitive when we visit someone else's house: we know what we like and, with luck, we're living in it already. I admit, though, I do get struck with moments of emerald green jealousy when I drive through the Cotswolds and see some of the loveliest domestic architecture in the world. Cottages have so much charm, a chocolate-box prettiness combined with the cosiness we need in our uncertain climate. Even though, once you're inside, the heavy thatch and small windows are inclined to make the rooms dark, they were obviously built to live in, rather than to impress the neighbours. And they are especially delightful in early summer, when the British, with their addiction to gardens, entwine them with roses and clematis.

I always yearned to own a thatched cottage, but my late husband forbade it. He grew up in one, and he said they are quite simply far too dangerous. A spark from a chimney can lie smouldering in the straw roof until, suddenly and ferociously, the whole roof is alight. The reason a cottage is so seductive is that it has the perfect quality of a home: as you walk through the door it seems to put its arms round you and you can nestle into it. (I assume nestle must come from 'nest' and that's exactly how it feels.) But you don't have to explore the furthest reaches of the English countryside to get that warm sensation.

Even crowded terrace houses crammed into Victorian industrial cities can feel just as cosy, spick and span, their front steps kept gleaming red by generations of meticulous housewives. I remember visiting Oldham in the seventies, when local councillors had declared great swathes of terrace houses 'unfit for human habitation' because they wanted to 'compulsorily purchase' them for twenty-five pounds each, demolish them and shove a new road across the wilderness they created. Not only did they destroy warm, vibrant communities, when I visited the houses themselves it was clear why they were nicknamed 'little palaces'. They had been so lovingly decorated, with brand-new bathrooms and rosy wallpaper. To see them being knocked down was to watch an act of unscrupulous vandalism. What have they been replaced with? We baby-boomers have watched the advance of the demolition men, seemingly inexorable in their determination to obliterate the old and replace it with the new. I remember walking through a Georgian square in London and seeing the ground scattered with ornate pieces of stucco and wood panelling. Now, where those gracious homes once stood, there are rectangular office blocks, shiny and soulless. The Victorian terraces of 'little palaces', where people chattered to their neighbours on their doorsteps and over their fences, have been replaced by towering blocks of concrete studded with glass and steel, where the wind blows along the balconies and graffiti bedeck the lifts. Politicians wonder why these estates are filled with crime, drugs and debt. Isn't it inevitable? These new flats aren't homes: people are enclosed and imprisoned in them, not nurtured. They become like battery hens, which notoriously peck themselves and each other to death. And when the only person who knocks on your door is the tally-man, or the door-to-door salesman, is it any wonder that lonely house-holders fall for their chat, and spend more than they have?

All too often city councillors treat their constituents worse than battery hens, more like their eggs, to be loaded into up-ended concrete egg boxes. I have yet to meet an architect who designed one of these vertical people-stackers and was prepared to live in it. No, they collect their fee and go home to their Georgian homes in the shires. And their victims, the inhabitants of the tower blocks, look bleakly out over city skylines, their children out of reach of any playgrounds or gardens. How can they climb a tree or dunk themselves in a river, when the nearest shivering plot of green surrounding their 'home' is filled with notices instructing 'No ball games' – indeed, no games of any kind? And then we wonder why the children on these bleak estates invent their own adventures, like vandalism and joy-riding. If it were up to me I'd insist that all our town planners spent a year in Samoa. You won't find an empty Coke can or plastic bag on the perfectly groomed roads and gardens on that idyllic Pacific island. Why? Because each village belongs to its inhabitants, literally, so if you spoil it, you're wrecking your own property. It's true communal living, and on a proper, human scale. Which means, of course, that everyone, child, parent or grandparent, is part of village life. But it's a distant dream to think we can recapture that warmth and vibrancy. So, how can we restore humanity and a human scale to the way too many of us live? For some of us, the answer is to take refuge with others of our own generation. Business is booming among those who create 'retirement villages'. Before you shudder, keep an open mind: it might suit you. A friend's parents, Max and Laura, had a house in Florida in one of these developments, and she thinks it extended both the quality and the length of their lives. Obviously they benefited from the warmth and the sunshine, but also from the friendship and fun they had there. Because of the particular population of Florida, mostly refugees from New York, Max and Laura were surrounded by retired producers and performers, migrating like birds of the brightest plumage each winter towards the sun. Every Christmas and Easter they put on spectacular amateur productions, usually of popular musicals. Since the shows were overseen by retired professionals, even though Maria and Jo were well into their seventies when they sang 'Tonight', shows like *West Side Story* were fun for the participants and for the audiences. Every day, they told me, was one long round of jollity, pool parties, bridge parties, cocktail parties, rounds of golf, gardening-club meetings, Scrabble marathons, whatever turned the inhabitants on. When I looked at the prospectus for a similar village to be built near Birmingham, I saw that its programme was much more British: it included woodwork, bell-ringing and abseiling.

There are solid advantages in this kind of housing. The managers specialise in providing excellent medical care on site, and good communal dining. By moving in, the residents also release valuable homes on to the housing market for young families to buy. So what is the downside? It's a ghetto designed for old people. This style of living really suits those who flinch when they hear a child's voice next to them on an aeroplane. For them, youth means noise, chaos, disruption and even danger. They find reassurance in being surrounded by elderly respectability, no loud music, no raves, no hoodies on street corners, plenty of time and company for the hobbies and interests they enjoy. It's an understandable choice, just not one I would make.

I prefer the Samoan style of life in a mixed neighbourhood, filled with the young, the old, the middle-aged. I know we can't live up to the South Pacific ideal of communal living. For me having a home in a North London suburb means I risk my life and my bumpers every morning as I try to compete with the school run. My streets are lined with fast-food stores and throwaway fashion shops, flashy and ephemeral, but isn't that rather fun? I enjoy the adrenalin and vitality of the London village I live in. The traffic may be a source of rage and stress, the coffee may be mass-produced and the jewellery shops may be crammed with junk, but still the heartbeat of my community is strong and compelling. What's more, I think, arrogantly, that I still have something to contribute. The bookshops, the theatre and the art cinema owe a great deal to my generation living there. And I think it's good for the young, even the very young, to grow up alongside the old. Otherwise they'll be so shielded from us that when old age comes upon them they'll be unprepared and terrified. Maybe it's due to my own childhood memories, my young life hugely enriched by the presence of grandparents and great-aunts, that I have no doubt I gained enormously from living alongside older people.

And now that I'm in my third age, I love the company of the young. Not exclusively, but as part of my everyday life. For me, the retirement village is too isolated from the rest of humanity. I'm not sure I embrace the idea that just because we share roughly the same birthdate we will have most other tastes in common. Oddly, I don't feel nearly as daunted by the thought of an old people's home as I do by a retirement village. I know that the time may come when I am so physically and mentally frail that I will have to depend on others to look after me. It's a frightening thought, when you hear stories of neglect and abuse. But I put beside those horror stories the visits I've made to busy, active homes where the residents are offered exercise and entertainment, and clearly enjoy each other's company. I hope, as I'm sure we all do, that I will be able to remain independent as long as possible, but if I can't, a well-run home is the obvious answer.

Until then, it's lovely to be in your own home,

surrounded by the bits and pieces you have collected over a long life. The house I live in is so crowded with happy ghosts and warm memories that I would leave it with the greatest reluctance. It is my home. The problem is, it is also a structure that I need to keep strong, sturdy and weather-proof. It is also the repository of most of my savings, so I need to maintain its value. My home is a house with its own needs, and it makes constant demands on me. As I write, I'm working out how to rebuild a garden wall that's beginning to totter, and prune the top of a couple of trees that are obscuring the view. There is a Forth Bridge aspect to an old house. Let's face it, the practical thing to do as we reach the foothills of old age, as long as we hang on to our health, is to move into a light, bright, newly purpose-built apartment. But to do that requires great self-discipline. You have to de-clutter. Throw away those musty old memories. Embrace the beige, if you can.

Step One. Take a clear, objective look at the stuff that clings like an obstinate barnacle to your life. Old clothes, for example. There's a wardrobe in my spare room that I never normally look inside, so recently I thought it would be a refreshing exercise to chuck out the tat accumulating there – things I'll certainly never wear again. A ridiculous white leather cowgirl outfit, for instance. I know Madonna brought back the Stetson, but nobody could revive a white fringed jacket and skirt with glued on sequins. Just as my hand was hovering over the bin, a memory stayed me. I wore that outfit in my one starring appearance in the Royal Variety Show in front of the Queen Mother, when a critic wrote, 'Esther sang "Anything you can do, I can do better," and proved she couldn't.' Maybe I should hang onto it to show my grandchildren. What about the navy blue Biba dress, so narrow I'll never get into it again? It's 45 years old, so it may become a valuable antique in another five years. The flimsy shirt I bought in Africa? No, that brings back precious memories of a family safari holiday. The Italian sundress that shows my nipples? Who knows, nipples may come back in style. You see how hopeless I am at closing the door to the past and moving on, even at emptying a wardrobe of garbage.

The same thing happened when an opportunity came to sell my London house. Out of the blue, without warning, a charming local lady fell in love with it, and offered me a princely sum for it. Logically I should have been thrilled. Instead, I thrashed around like a salmon on a hook. It was so obviously a good idea that my accountant was in seventh heaven. But I had nowhere else in London to go to. My estate agent took me to visit some of the minimalist chrome and glass apartments I could have afforded, had I sold up, and I had to admit they were cleverly planned, and some had spectacular views. What was wrong with them? They weren't home. The charming lady's patience ran out, rightly, and she bought somewhere else. But in her wake the estate agent brought other potential purchasers to my door. Out of my hearing, he reported that one snooty lady said to another, 'I don't mind the price they're asking, but for that money you'd expect it to be done already.'

Done? Whatever did she mean? What was there to 'do', for heaven's sake? I tried to look at my lovely, shabby-chic house through her eyes. My kitchen floor is tiled with brick-red quarry tiles, the work surfaces are wood, the paintwork is olive green. To me that makes it a perfect country-style kitchen with an original fireplace, the sills filled with flowers, a room big enough to cook, eat and socialise in. What could be better? I'll tell you. The wood should be replaced with black granite. The quarry tiles should be covered with pale gold limestone. The sinks, instead of sensible taps that turn on and off, should have levers that rock, with sink plugs that pop up and down. The drawers should be replaced with baskets. The serviceable but elderly dishwasher and oven should be replaced. Instead of the John Piper print of convolvulus and petunias over the mantelpiece I should have a flat plasma TV screen. In other words, I should buy all the interior-decoration magazines and slavishly copy them. Now I think about it, I recognise that my dining room is even worse than my kitchen. It's filled with relics of my first home with Desmond: rosewood veneer table and sideboards, the much scorned 'brown furniture'. Over the table hangs an antique lamp rifled from an old church. This week I heard the president of the RIBA castigating the builders' merchants of the sixties for selling 'curly brass'. Every lamp in my house is 'curly brass'. Clearly

I should turf all that out, and replace it with steel and plastic. My dining room should be furnished with a smoked-glass table, and chrome and leather chairs. I should tear down the chintz swags and tails around the window and put up a slatted blind instead. Out with the Chinese water-colours, souvenirs of my son's gap year spent teaching in a Chinese school, and up with abstract blocks of colour on my walls instead. Dump the memories, the sentimentality. No more 'curly brass'. Replace it all with new, shiny, machine-turned IKEA products, their functional, clean lines disinfected of nostalgia. Yuck. And so it goes on, throughout my rambling Georgian home. The practical blue stair-carpet must be ripped up; only beige will do nowadays. The Victorian furniture in the hall must go. I'll have to invest in more chrome and glass, build slatted covers for the radiators, and hang modern mirrors on the walls. I have far too much chintz, too many pictures, a plethora of family photographs; out they would have to go, if I were to please would-be purchasers. But that's the big question: is it really what I want to do? The answer is, partly. Some rooms in my house are purely functional so I have no regrets about throwing out stuff that has been accumulating there over the years. Bit by bit I have reformed my old-fashioned bathrooms, tiling the floors and smartening up the loos. When we bought the house twenty years ago I liked the elderly equipment: it reminded me of my grandmother's house and had a kind of industrial archaeological charm. I could visualise a local museum asking me for my cloakroom wash-basin. But as time went by, I had to admit that we all, as Anita Loos put it, lose our charms in the end. So now my cloakroom and bathrooms are the requisite white, with beige walls and marbled sand-coloured tiled floors. I can't pretend the transition was painless. For at least a month after a cowboy installed the new equipment there were leaks and blockages until I hired another army of plumbers to put the previous bodging right. Now everything gleams and, what's more, it works.

I know how expensive and worrying all this can be, but I recommend you do the same, if your sinks, loos, baths and showers are as decrepit as mine were. There is nothing more depressing than an 'old lady's flat' where spiders lurk in the corners and the sun don't shine. The trouble is, once you get used to the new, clean look, you may start feeling discontented with the gathering grime in the rest of the house. But don't go too far, if you want to keep your sanity (or your dog). I have a friend who has laid cream carpet throughout her home. I tiptoe when I visit her. One day, I suppose, when my stairs become as intimidating as the Himalayas, and my trees become a jungle, I will want to sell my home and buy that practical newly built flat. Then I have resolved that I will call in the painters and turn my currently blue-and-gold house beige from roof to basement (although, who knows?, by then the fashion will be pink or purple). I'll call in the removal firm, take out every stick of furniture I own, and each picture, and replace it with hired trendiness. So the next time snooty ladies call, they'll find my darling home has been well and truly 'done'. But until that day comes, wherever my eyes rest there is a treasured memory. It may be tat to you, and I know that the day I die my treasures will turn instantly into junk. But until then, my house is my home, and I like it that way.

Chapter Fifteen

Technology

> " *Always do what you are afraid to do* "

Ralph Waldo Emerson

The stereotype is that we who are over forty have an overriding fear of new technology. As one charming and, of course, very young lady *Breakfast* news presenter put it to me, 'As you get older, you think more slowly, so you can't keep up with modern means of communication.'

'Bollocks,' I retorted, proving her point. Had I been thinking fast enough I would have censored myself.

But she caught me on a raw nerve. All too often we baby-boomers are accused of resenting change for its own sake. The truth is that although we may not like change when there's no reason for it, and we may distrust the urge automatically to turf out anything more than ten years old, show us the advantages and we will be the first to embrace new techniques and technology.

How do I know? Recently the Institute of Lifelong Learning conducted a survey of older people in the workplace. Guess what? The response proved that younger colleagues by an overwhelming majority regarded them as skilled, experienced, conscientious, reliable, loyal and eager to embrace new skills. So there. A moment's thought will work out why this should be. We older workers appreciate the opportunity to work whether it's because we need the money or because we like the challenge and we enjoy working alongside the young. We are determined to make the work itself enjoyable and successful. We are long past the stage of wanting to rule the world, and (unless we happen to be built on the same ferocious and voracious model as a Mao Tse Tung or Robert Mugabe) no longer driven by the burning ambition that is such a fiery crucible for the young. It has been replaced by the desire for quality of life, rather than quantity of bank balance. We want to enjoy each moment. And that includes each moment at work. So show us a piece of new technology that improves our quality of life and increases our skills, and we will embrace it whole-heartedly. After all, we are the generation that has been familiar with the fruits of the industrial revolution from the moment we were born. I happened to be a Caesarean baby, and so was my younger sister. You may recall that Macduff was from his mother's womb untimely ripped, which he survived but his mum didn't. That, tragically, used to be standard for Caesarean babies: our passport to life was our mother's death certificate. However, by my time, thank heaven and modern medicine, that had changed. I was brought up to believe (but have no proof) that the Queen Mother and mine have this in common; Queen Elizabeth and Katherine Rantzen had two daughters each, both born by Caesarean section, both surviving, as did their mothers. The reason my mother had the operations was thanks to another piece of scientific equipment, the X-ray, which revealed it was the only way that the three of us, my sister, my mother and I, could possibly survive childbirth. And the operation was only available to us because, back in the nineteenth century, anaesthesia had been invented. So my sister, the Queen and I were all born into, and thanks to, the age of technology.

My own life, and I guess yours too, continued to be saved thanks to modern inventions and discoveries. At the age of eight, in 1948, I developed a serious illness that would have killed me had I caught it ten years earlier. It was an acute kidney disease, nephritis, which was cured by doctors at University College Hospital in London using a very early type of penicillin. Alexander Fleming had only recently, in 1928, discovered that a stray mould on one of his petri dishes was knocking off the staphylococcus bacteria there. Then, in the 1940s, two medical researchers isolated penicillin and turned it into a powder, which was taken straight to the battlefields, where it did sterling work saving soldiers' lives. After the war, it was applied to hospital patients like eight-year-old me in 1948. I can't pretend I enjoyed it. At that time penicillin was a thick concoction that had to be injected into my thighs and buttocks via a needle normally used on horses. I was black and blue with bruises by the end of three months, but I was cured. Thanks to technology. Of all the medical discoveries, and we seem to be making them every day, antibiotics must be among the most dramatic. Certainly I am one of billions of people who owe their lives to them. I came out of hospital in May, and I'll never forget my first sight of a huge plane tree in a London square, in full, glorious, green leaf. After the dirty brick streets, which had been the only view from the hospital ward, it looked spectacular. That tree, for me, is still the symbol of life. I returned to a home that, even back in 1948, was already pretty technological. Gone were the days of carbolic soap and washing boiled in coppers. We had electricity, gas and constant hot water. In our home we had wirelesses, wonderful Bakelite constructions, some plugged into the wall, others battery-driven, on which we could listen to the nine o'clock news and the King's speech on Christmas Day. In our scullery we even had a fridge, quite bad-tempered and not terribly glamorous, but functional and filled with free-range eggs, then the only variety available. Technology in 1948 had not yet reached the animals in British farmyards, thank goodness, though there were plenty of tractors in the fields. However, on our first holidays to France we marvelled at the medieval sight of oxen pulling ploughs.

Maybe we were a particularly adventurous family because my father, a pioneering electrical engineer working for the BBC, had one of the first televisions in the world. I remember with affection the tiny white dot that slowly dwindled in the centre of the screen, like a dying star, when we turned it off. We had a car – in fact, my grandmother had bought one of the first cars fifty years earlier, and was taught to drive by her groom, who cannily kept the passenger door open so he could jump out if necessary, and shouted, 'Whoa!' if he felt her speed was exceeding fifteen miles an hour. After the war she drove a lovely Armstrong Siddeley limousine, kitted out in leather and walnut, with its own picnic basket in the boot. She certainly didn't shy away from technology.

But, then, the Victorians and Edwardians in Britain had never been cowed by new ideas: they took their inventions proudly around the world, and my generation inherited that sense of pride and adventure. I won't say there weren't cul-de-sacs and eccentricities. My father was a professional inventor working to develop early television, but when he brought his skills home, the results were sometimes quaint. Appalled by the tannin stains in the spout of our teapot, he invented the spoutless teapot. We applauded, even though we secretly thought he'd reinvented the jug. When we bought a wall-mounted electric fire, he was concerned that pulling its string to turn it on and off might bring it down upon us, so instead of mounting it on the wall bracket intended for it, he welded it to a piece of flexible metal that sent it juddering up and down for several minutes, and kept our school-friends amused at teatime.

When he was seconded to the United Nations head-quarters at Lake Success, New York, to take charge of their telecommunications, we were surrounded in our domestic life by more technology than we had dreamed of. Far bigger American refrigerators meant my mother only had to visit the local supermarket in the shopping mall (paradise to deprived British eyes, used to the bleakness of ration-book England in the fifties) once a week. There were washing-machines and tumble-dryers, so my mother's mangle could take a rest until we returned to London, and drive-in movies, which meant all kinds of romance were possible for 'bobby-soxers' in the back seats of huge gas-guzzling American cars.

Of course, the concept of gas-guzzling had not been invented in those pre-Lovelockian days. (James Lovelock was the visionary who first perceived the real ecological cost of the industrial revolution. He diagnosed the problem, that every aspect of the earth's climate, its animal, vegetable and mineral makeup, is interdependent: tip the balance too far one way, and catastrophe ensues. In his eighties he wrote his deeply pessimistic treatise *The Revenge of Gaia*. If ever there were proof that the old are still ahead of the game, he provides it. I heartily recommend it, though I can't pretend it's a cheerful read.) But back in the fifties we had no idea we were living in the planetary equivalent of the *Titanic*. We had machines, 'labour-saving devices' that we came to rely on. In the charming white clapboard house we lived in on the North Shore of Long Island there was not only central heating (I had grown up in bedrooms in Cricklewood where in winter there was ice inside the windows), but air-conditioning was also standard. The food mixers and juicers took the hard labour out of cookery, and so did the cake mixes, with their luscious frostings. In Miracle Mile, a shopping mall built thirty years before they were born or thought of in Britain, we seemed to have entered a paradise of obedient machinery that enhanced our lives without costing us anything but the sum on the price tag (nobody had yet worked out the cost to the planet). So my childhood, partly because of my father's job, partly through our two years spent on Long Island, New York, familiarised me with the pleasures and advantages of technology.

So did sex. The inescapable truth is that sex was intended

to create babies. If we want to frustrate that intention, we need technology. Rubber, or plastic, served that purpose for years. Then in the sixties came the invention that changed the world, particularly for us young women. It was, of course, the pill. We don't often bring up the subject in front of today's young: they'd screw up their noses with revulsion at the thought that people with wrinkles could ever have made love, but we were the first generation to enjoy anxiety-free sex. What a foolish sentence that is. What Erica Jong called 'the zipperless fuck' never did exist, and never will. The invention of the pill simply transfers the responsibility, but can't take it away. Good sex bonds people together. Bad sex is a trauma. Yes, of course we can have light-hearted sex, just for fun, but drunken sex erodes the soul. That may sound irremediably Puritanical, but what the hell? I've lived long enough, seen and heard enough to feel I can justify my views.

So, back in the sixties when the pill became commonly available, it caused a good deal of heart-searching. I remember the earnest conversations with my friends: should we take the pill even though there was no real relationship in our lives? Would that make us more likely to have the stupid, shaming one-night stand or less? I never much liked the idea of chemically interfering with such a basic hormonal function, so I stayed with the more primitive methods of contraception far longer than my friends did, and even today I'm not sure there isn't a 'pill shadow': so many of my pill-using friends had trouble subsequently in conceiving when they wanted to. But that may just have been due to the fact that now women can chemically defer having babies until their careers allow, which often means waiting until they are in their late thirties, or early forties; by that time their fertility has dropped, so conception can be difficult.

The pill was not alone in changing humanity physically and mentally. It belonged to a tradition of fundamental changes brought about for us, men and women, by scientists in their laboratories. George Washington had false teeth created for him, but his were made of wood, not terrifically comfortable, and I imagine his smile lost some of its original charm. I have the modern equivalent, a few titanium implants in my gums, which not only improve my chewing capacity, but my corpse will have added value. Benjamin Franklin (another example of the American ingenuity when it came to gadgetry), back in the eighteenth century, created a pair of bi-focal eyeglasses because he was tired of having to change his spectacles, and I have had silicone implants in my eyes, which mean I'll never suffer from cataracts, as my grandmother did.

Speaking of implants, cosmetic surgery has created a real revolution, so that synthetic breasts and buttocks are becoming commonplace. And alongside such frippery there are the medical transformations of old age, artificial ankle, knee and hip joints, heart bypasses, and kidney transplants. We in our senior years are becoming more and more familiar with the advantages of medical science and technology. So, thanks to gadgets, machines, chemistry and physics, the lucky among us are spryer and more physically able than any previous third-agers. And thanks also to technology, if it does become more difficult for us to leave the comfort of our homes, we now have a huge range of entertainment literally at our fingertips. At first micro-chip manufacturers made a fundamental error when they created home entertainment for us. The early video recorders were so complex they required a child of ten to understand and operate them; they were far too intricate for anyone older to master. But the designers have mended their ways, and now even adults can order over the Internet any kind of music, or DVD, or even that quaint old-fashioned form of entertainment, the book, if our fancy lights upon it.

My sister, now living in Australia, sends me my favourite chocolates and flowers on special occasions, and they arrive on time and exactly according to her choice, thanks to the world-wide web. I no longer curse when I miss my favourite programmes, because my television automatically finds and records them for me, and even if I decide after the event that I would have enjoyed a particular show I had missed, I can always download a podcast of it on to my computer. I haven't quite thrown away my collection of CDs yet, though I know they are very much a relic of the last century, in order to rely upon my iPod, but that day isn't far away. I still enjoy going to our local cinema when there's a film several of us want to see together because that's a treat and I like the shared experience of joining an audience. But if the multi-screens insist on offering noisome-smelling snacks, mainly involving wraps filled with curry, which waft round our local cinema until it reeks, I may retreat, as many of the young already have, to my solitary screen at home. I suspect we, the print and paper generation, will miss the experience of looking up some subject in an encyclopaedia. Wikipedia, the naughty, anarchic Internet jumble of references is not nearly as satisfying, or as authoritative. Our family *Encyclopaedia Britannica* used grandly to fill the specially made cherrywood bookcase that was sold with it, and we used to love the ritual of asking an abstruse question then leafing through the dense pages to find the answer. I was, however, slightly off-put by the memory of a tea-party I had endured with my least favourite don in my last year at university.

Miss Lascelles was tiny, white-haired, meticulous and ferocious. She never betrayed any interest in, or affection for, the young who were her students. I remember a friend of mine timidly reading an essay to her, as we were required to each fortnight, to be greeted with the one-word critique, 'No.' I was amazed, when I handed mine in, for it to be handed back to me with the comment, 'I must congratulate you, Miss Rantzen, on your writing.' For a moment I thought she meant my style. 'Very legible,' she said, dashing my hopes. So, when the invitation to tea arrived for four of us at the end of our university career, we accepted with dread. Tea was specified as being at four fifteen, so we thought it would be polite to arrive at four twenty. We were wrong. As we rang the bell the door sprang open, like a jack-in-the-box (remember them?), and Miss Lascelles greeted us in her delicate, chiming, upper-class voice: 'Ah, here you are, at last. I'll just go and warm the scones up again.'

We ate them as silently as possible, crumbling them on to our plates, as she told us this story. 'Last Thursday evening,' she said, 'there was a full, round pale moon in the sky. And I heard a ring at my doorbell. When I went to the front door, there was a small man standing on my doorstep with a full, round pale face. He said to me, "Good evening, madam. Would you care to purchase a copy of the *Encyclopaedia Britannica?*" I said, "No, thank you." He said, 'Would your children care for a copy of the *Encyclopaedia Britannica?*' I said, "I have no children, and I am at present writing the *Encyclopaedia Britannica.*"' And she was, at least the entry for Jane Austen, which I wasn't able to consult for years without feeling the dry crumbs of those scones in my mouth.

Technology has altered many of our relationships, for better and worse. Transport, by cars, trains and planes, has meant that the old, comfortable communities and extended families are shattered and dispersed. Gone are the days (only Dickens's time, in the mid-nineteenth century) when a journey of two hundred miles took an intimidating twenty-four hours by stagecoach. The effect of the speed and (sometimes) comfort of modern transport has been dramatic. My family are scattered now around the world. So the telephone and the Internet has leaped into the breach if we are to stay in touch, and at least that means we can communicate instantly via emails, while the young adore the social networking sites like Facebook and Bebo.

The pessimists predict that the young will forget entirely how to make conversation and meet someone's eyes across a crowded room, that they'll be doing it all in cyber-space instead. Well, they said that about fast food and microwaves: nutritionists gloomily predicted that nobody would be able to boil an egg in a few years' time. And in a way they have been proved right: the fast-food industry has created an epidemic of obesity. And yet at the same time there has never been such a boom in broadcasts and publications devoted to food; there is a plethora of celebrity cooks and cookery competitions, with much emphasis on obscure ingredients and yet new gadgetry, so someone somewhere must be juicing and whizzing, wok-ing and baking and making up new recipes.

We need to eat, drink, hold on to our families, make friends and find lovers. So my guess is that, like the food industry, the relationship trades will discover ways of allowing new inventions to flourish alongside the old, and that the two will complement each other. We will just use the Internet to stay in touch with old friends and far-flung relatives. There is no doubt that computers themselves are changing and will continue to change radically. It feels wasteful, all this instant obsolescence. I remember sitting in my BBC office and watching electric typewriters fall from the offices above into a waiting skip. They were almost new, and it was shockingly destructive, but the microchip had meant they were suddenly completely useless. I'm sure the same will happen to my nice new lightweight computer. My friend Bryher, who introduced me to my much-loved hybrid petrol and electric Toyota Prius, now tells me that computers in the future will look like a piece of material you simply unfold, and on a screen as light and portable as a sheet of paper you will search out your entertainment, your communication, your bank account, the lot. She tells me that, quite soon, our screens will either be big or small, depending on whether we want to sit back and watch, or sit forward and use. That soon some multi-billionaire will master the skill of taking micro-payments from us all, which will revolutionise selling via the Internet, and that will be how the currently fragile newspaper, broadcasting and music industries will fund themselves.

The ways we heat our homes and businesses, and transport ourselves will change radically too, as all the energy sources we used to rely on run out (except nuclear energy, of course, but there we have the problem of where to put it once we've used it). We will have to find new ones, if we are to hang on to what we call civilisation. Which maybe we won't, in which case perhaps we will face extinction, and become the dinosaurs of our own time. At least my dentist will be immortal. As long as I have the foresight to keel over into a peat bog, archaeologists of the future will be poring over my titanium implants in a museum in the distant future. If I die at all, that is. One of the other prophecies, closer than teleporting, time travel or the cloak of invisibility, is that medical science will soon find the way to turn back the clock and reverse the ageing process. You and I may be among the first generation to live for ever. The fountain of youth, instead of a wild dream, will become a reality. And here your guess is, of course, as good as mine. I assume that for space reasons the human race will have to stop producing new babies, and old people, now newly young again, will take over the world. Certain changes will be instantaneous, and to the good. Raucous music will cease. Fast food will go out of business. Alcopops will be no more. Theatre will have a renaissance, especially the classic works of Shakespeare, Shaw, Sheridan and Agatha Christie. Cinemas will stop making high-school movies, and start making witty, stylish comedies instead, so that Emma Thompson can become the new Audrey Hepburn. The BBC news will go back to nine o'clock, and let *News at Ten* take its rightful place at ten.

It is tempting to believe that a world dominated by the elderly will regain its taste and dignity, and lose the trashy garbage that currently offends us. But a world without the young is a horrific thought. If we lost their thrusting irreverence, what would really happen to the world? Would we as a species lose the impulse to explore and push our way across accepted boundaries? Would we become conservative, cling to the world we know, resist new discoveries? I hope not.

I began this chapter with Emerson's advice always to do what we are afraid to do. Which doesn't mean we should all rush towards inventions when our own experience tells us that's likely to be foolhardy. But we do need to hang on to a sense of adventure, resisting the temptation to surrender to suspicion or dread just because something is unfamiliar. We baby-boomers, the 'silver surfers' who, we are told, are now the majority Internet users, embrace the good things we recognise technology brings us, while resisting what we have reason to believe may be fatal to humanity. But if you're looking into a crystal ball, and you believe James Lovelock, his advice would be to enjoy technology while we can, and if possible, move to Oslo. Because, thanks to climate change, he says, everywhere else is like the edge of the Niagara Falls, and we are all in our little technological pleasure boat heading towards it, without the least idea that the engine is about to fail.

Chapter Sixteen

Memory

"Why is it that our memory is good enough to retain the least triviality that happens to us, yet not good enough to recollect how often we have told it to the same person?"

La Rochefoucauld

Our memory, according to a recent edition of the BBC's *Horizon*, is our self, who we are. According to the fascinating scientific research explored in the programme, until we have a sense of self, and can recognise our own face in a mirror, we have no memory. It's like beads which need a string to hang on before they can become a necklace. Or individual notes that need a melody to become a song. If we accept that thesis, then the longer our memories, the more individual we become. And since my view, expressed in every chapter of this book, is that older is better, some of that improvement must be due to the richness of experience stored away in our long-term memories. Of course, there are downsides of the ageing process. The *Horizon* programme also repeated the depressing statistic that when we reach forty, ten thousand of our brain cells are dying each day, that our memory is at its peak when we are twenty-five, and that from the age of twenty-seven it begins to fade. But it also pointed out that, provided we are not cursed with illnesses like Alzheimer's, or other forms of brain damage and disease, we will find ways of compensating for the loss of all those cells. I don't miss them at all. It's a bit like the clutter in my house: those cells are just a load of stuff. It may reassure me to have heaps of dead leaves from the forest of my past around me, but do I really need them? Would it really concern me if they were swept up and taken away, with all my unnecessary brain cells?

But there is one specific loss, unnoticed by *Horizon*, but all too obvious to me. From some time in my forties, I lost the capacity to store any new names in my brain. That matters. In his book *How to Win Friends and Influence People*, Dale Carnegie wrote, 'Remember that a man's name is to him the sweetest and most important sound in the English language.' Though I may remember the advice, I have lost the ability to follow it. Once upon a time I could. For much of my early life I had a reasonably good memory for names. But past forty I found a black hole had opened up in my mind, and gradually every proper noun I ever knew began to fall into it. I battled against the loss. My head-mistress, who remembered the name of every child she had ever taught, showed me how flattering and impressive that skill is.

A friend who attended a lunch with Bill Clinton told me that when they were first introduced he not only knew her name but her son's too. He obviously recalled it from his briefing, because he mentioned her son without prompting from her, and autographed a photograph specifically for him. She remembered Clinton's skill, with awe. And although she recognised it for what it was, the professional ability to use a photographic memory, the implied compliment was infinitely flattering. She felt that she and her son had registered on this famous man's mind, he who had met so many far more celebrated people in his time. Whereas I have just received an abusive note from a woman who felt I had grievously insulted her by not introducing her when we both attended a charity event. It wasn't that I wouldn't, it was that I couldn't. Her name had disappeared into that deep, black hole in my brain.

I am not alone in this new disability. Shortly after I turned fifty I held a dinner party for a dozen of my contemporaries.

The conversation around the table was filled with lacunae. 'Did you see Whatsername in that play at the Youknow, the theatre at the end of Thing Street?' Every proper noun had been extinguished, snuffed out by age. If you are a fellow sufferer, I can offer one tip that might be useful: I've learned that the worst way to summon a name is to pursue it like a ferret chasing a rabbit down its burrow. It simply refuses to come out. Instead you have to change the subject, walk away, figuratively speaking, and as soon as you have turned your back that missing word will creep out into the sunshine. Then grab it quick, before it hides again.

Another fascinating fact, which may explain much about our own conversation, let alone our friends' story-telling, is that each time we retrieve a memory, we put it back slightly altered. It's as if we took a pair of socks out of their drawer, tried them on, pulled them slightly out of shape, or wore a hole in the toe, then put them back. That explains why I sometimes add someone else's detail to my account of an event we both remember; their colour or anecdote glues itself to my memory. Many raconteurs rely on this syndrome. My late husband Desmond Wilcox was famous for the way his stories kept improving with the retelling. They say David Niven profited from the same process, hence the popularity of his autobiographies, which were crammed with polished and repolished anecdotes. At which point, let me give you an instance of one of Desmond's stories, which he told to an entranced audience of television colleagues over a glass of wine in his office. 'In the sixties,' he told us, 'I was at a wild Chelsea party, and I remember Laurence Olivier standing naked on the mantelpiece, while the rest of us tried to throw bagels at him so that they hooked themselves on his personal anatomy.' We, Desmond's audience, went cross-eyed trying to visualise the nation's finest actor naked wearing only a bagel. Desi looked at us with satisfaction, then had a moment of doubt, and asked, 'Or do I mean Oliver Reed?' He did. Once again, the proper nouns had evaded his memory.

I have no doubt someone has invented some brain exercise which is supposed to compensate for this loss, but I'd be surprised if it works. The noted neurologist Baroness Susan Greenfield, in her fascinating television series about the human brain, cited the case of a man who had suffered damage to the crucial part of the brain where facial recognition is stored. A picture of Marilyn Monroe was put in front of him. He was completely baffled. 'She's blonde, very famous in the fifties, she sang "Happy Birthday" to President Kennedy,' the researcher told him. At once he knew exactly who it was. 'Marilyn Monroe,' he said confidently. But even though she was arguably the best-known icon of the century, he couldn't recognise her simply by looking at her.

I can sympathise. Every day someone I meet will say, 'You don't remember me.' Sometimes I know we've met, but I fumble around in my mind until they remind me of the context of that meeting. There are a few exceptions, people who for some quirk of my memory engraved themselves indelibly upon it. Five years ago in East Anglia I was lecturing to an audience when a young woman in the front row asked, 'Who is the craziest person you ever met? Before you answer that, Esther, I should tell you that I'm sitting next to my mother, who used to eat wood.'

'Christine!' I shouted with joy. I'm not really surprised that I remembered Christine, even though I interviewed many unusual people during the twenty-one years *That's Life!* was on the air. There was a man who fell in love with frogs, and insisted on sitting next to one and kissing it while he talked to me. There was a woman who cooked steak on the manifold of her car when she went out for a drive. And several men had such productive relationships with their pets that one taught his dog to read, another got his horse to count, a farmer played a tune on the udder clusters of milking machines, and a pair of identical twins banged tunes on each other's skull with spanners. But even among such a varied crowd of English eccentrics Christine was outstanding. She ran through her local park, nibbling the bark of different trees, and became so expert she could tell the *Daily Mirror* from the *Sun* by the taste of the wood pulp used to make the paper. So I can understand why she engraved herself on my memory. But why did I remember her name, when I have, only once but memorably, forgotten my own nephew's?

'Agnosia' is the medical term for some of the odd syndromes that affect the memory, like the man who couldn't name Marilyn. It seems there are many specific disabilities, usually caused by brain damage, which prevent us recognising people or things, even when we can see and describe them quite clearly. For example, some people lose the capacity to recognise a voice, even when they hear it distinctly and can understand exactly what is being said. Others have excellent hearing, but can't understand the words. Some people have music agnosia: they hear the different notes, but not as music. Or mirror agnosia, which knocks out objects to the left or right, or there's even 'finger agnosia'. These are rare disabilities. For most of us, the filing system in our minds works fairly well, and allows us to collect the treasures we want to hoard so that at some time in the future we can retrieve them. Why don't we keep everything? Some experts believe that we forget on purpose the unpleasant or boring things we hope we will never need, and therefore don't want to remember. But like many systems, our mental files are unpredictable. I used to work on a radio programme which broadcast live very early on Monday mornings, called *Start the Week with Richard Baker*. The late John Peel once took part in it. Much later he wrote a piece criticising me, I thought unfairly, so I wrote to him protesting that we had never met. He replied, icily, that we had indeed, early one Monday morning in a radio studio. It can't have helped our relationship that I hadn't the slightest memory of that meeting. I could have blamed the hour, or the time of the week, or my preoccupation with my own contribution. But it wouldn't be true. We hadn't taken to each other so I must have shredded the memory. On the other hand, I do remember meeting on the same programme one of my heroes, the great lyricist Johnny Mercer, who wrote the fabulous line in 'Moon River', 'my huckleberry friend'. Clearly that was such a treasured memory that I have stored it somewhere handy where I can take it out and gloat over it whenever I want to.

The theory that we store what we like, and discard what we don't is disproved by the obvious fact that many of the memories that haunt us are not at all pleasant. PTSD, post-traumatic stress disorder, is now recognised as a very common phenomenon. Sufferers don't simply have to live through the original ordeal, but they must relive it in flashbacks and nightmares. When ChildLine opened in 1986, I heard stories of incredible suffering told by the adult survivors of child abuse who had never spoken of their pain before. I became only too aware that they were totally unhealed, and that the terrible events seemed to have happened only a day or two earlier, they were so fresh in the memory, and had been relived so often. Modern medicine is trying to find effective ways to erase these disabling memories, using psychotherapy, hypnotherapy and drugs, such as beta-blockers, with some success. But it is a conundrum that our brains seem compelled to preserve traumas that torment us, while they insist on dumping memories we value and would find useful.

There is, of course, a distinction between the long-term and the short-term 'working' memory. They are stored in different parts of the brain, and transferred from one to the other if we need them, a process that seems to happen in our sleep. When I was working on regular television programmes and had to absorb detailed facts, figures and the profiles of many interviewees (sometimes seventy different guests in a day), I managed to train my short-term memory to retain briefly but accurately the information I needed for each show, but then to erase it all from my mental tape so it was fresh, clean and empty again. When I was writing and producing *That's Life!*, I knew every detail of the script by the time we broadcast the weekly show. At the last minute the final version was typed on to the prompting device 'Autocue'. One Sunday night, just before I had to read it live to the audience, the normally unflappable operator cut the wrong paragraph. To my own astonishment, under the intoxicating influence of adrenalin, I spoke the paragraph that should have been unrolling before my eyes but wasn't as I watched her spool desperately through the paragraph that shouldn't have been there but was. No way could I have done that in my right mind, or in rehearsal. I did it because I was on the special 'high' created by performance, and my short-term memory was on overdrive. The effect never lasted. The very next day, after a night's sleep, I had forgotten every line of that script, and many of the salient facts, because week after week my brain erased my mental tape of everything it had decided I would never need again.

The performance high isn't always helpful to the memory. It totally sabotaged my attempts to learn the rumba and the tango when I appeared in *Strictly Come Dancing*. I've never been any good at learning dance steps. Had I been to ballet classes when I was a toddler, perhaps that experience would have trained my brain but, alas, I was as round as a peanut, so my mother kindly excused me. In my sixties the need for this new skill suddenly arose because I was invited to take part in the fabulous TV show that has swept the world. In three weeks' rehearsal beforehand I was able to master the waltz so that I just about got away with it. But as the pace hotted up, the next two dances we had to learn in a week were quite beyond me. Each time I tried to learn the sensual steps of the rumba and the tango, it was as if my brain was overruling and paralysing my muscle memory. Even when I thought I had learned the choreography, the adrenalin of live transmission blotted it out. As we walked down the glamorous staircase to the dance floor, my partner, Anton du Beke, kept tight hold of my wrist because he knew, faced with the total blank in my cerebral cortex, I was likely to cut and run. I did ask permission to take a small glass of wine just before the broadcast, to see if that would help, but the producer refused to allow it. Health and Safety regulations forbade it. Although I was voted off the show after three editions, I loved the experience, and gained a great deal from it. It was so different from any programme I had ever tried to make that it totally altered my mental approach, and my posture.

One of the many pieces of advice handed out by the expert and less expert on the Internet and in the media, if we want to hang on to such mental capacity as remains to us, is to keep doing new and different things, and learning new skills. The most recent trend has been the games that call themselves brain trainers. As I was depressed to find one of these machines assessed my mental age as ninety-four, I decided not to invest in one. My own favourite exercises are Scrabble, combined with the occasional cryptic crossword. But plenty of tips are published in the media on the best way to improve a failing memory. Sadly I've forgotten what they are. That is, of course, because in my case I could never make them work.

I have interviewed dozens of freakish geniuses who could remember exactly in what order cards were arranged in a pack, or the names of every member of a studio audience of two hundred, and did it by visualising them in some strange pathway through a forest. I respected the fact that it did the trick for them, but I could never make it work for me. However, another formative experience was a series in which I took part to be taught French by the 'immersion method', in other words, by being forced to speak only

French for a month, from nine in the morning until six at night. I had reached A-level standard at school, but then, at the age of nineteen, I stopped speaking French entirely, out of fear that I would make terrible blunders in grammar and vocabulary. Since forty-five years had gone by, and I was sixty-five by the time I made the programme, the gifted young people producing it assumed I must have forgotten all I knew. What they failed to understand is that sixty-five-year-olds remember very clearly what they did at nineteen: it's last week that defeats them. Long term, OK, short term, dodgy. So, as French came back to me more and more easily, the production team was forced to try and make my life as difficult as possible by setting challenges for me, like having to act as a waitress in a snooty French restaurant, or interviewing a senior French politician live on television, or finding my way to a tiny island off the coast in the pouring rain, all of which stretched me to the limit. Which was why it was so good for my ageing brain cells. That programme taught me far more than I had anticipated about the workings of the elderly brain. Songs, poems, plays and fables I hadn't remembered for half a century, originally taught me by my remarkable French teacher, Caroline Senator (you see how I have no trouble at all remembering her name? Just don't ask me who is the current Secretary of State for Defence), drifted back into my mind, as if the last forty or fifty years had preserved them perfectly until the moment arrived to bring them out into the sunshine again.

Singing the songs of Georges Brassens in my bath of a morning, as I did, suddenly I was a teenager again, wandering along the banks of the Seine, sipping a paper cup of mulled wine and brushing the sugar from a warm doughnut off my chin. That summer of 1957 was yesterday again, clear, vivid and delightful. I even remembered the name of the tall, dark, romantic French boy who was with me that evening, Maurice Douek. I wonder where he is now?

Music is particularly evocative. The BBC's Radio 2 offers a real service to us baby-boomers, playing the songs we loved in our teens and twenties. I'm sure the pleasure of hearing them again lowers our blood pressure, and revives our hearts. My uncle Max, in his nineties, loves conducting the CD his daughter Judy made for him, with music-hall songs he can sing along to. And, of course, listening to the songs of his youth makes him feel young again, the gleam in his eyes, and the smile on his face telling their own story. For many years now, reminiscence therapy has been accepted as beneficial to the elderly. Sometimes formalised, with scrap-books and videos of the period of their youth, often less formal, with young volunteers selected to visit older people and ask them questions about times gone by. But I think this may be something we could and should do for ourselves, and our families. Why not jot down the memories of our own times, and put together a collection of the books we read, the music we listened to, the films and programmes we enjoyed when we were young? I'm not for a moment suggesting that we should live in the past, only that we can give our memories an enjoyable workout and at the same time fascinate our children and grandchildren. (And if they're not fascinated, they should be.)

Why restrict ourselves to our own lifetimes? A friend of mine discovered some letters from her great-grandfather when he travelled across the Midwest of the United States. My sister consulted the Internet and found some valuable websites she has used to research our ancestry. And I have had the wonderful experience of taking part in the BBC's *Who Do You Think You Are?* To say this last was a life-changing experience is an understatement. It changed my view of myself and of the world. Speaking to other people whose family history has been unearthed by the researchers for the series, I know that for most of them it has also been a revelation. Some have had family legends shattered. It must be devastating to have believed all your life that you are Scottish, as Alistair McGowan, the brilliant impressionist did, and then suddenly to discover that you are Anglo-Indian, and that your ancestors were Irish. Television newsreader Natasha Kaplinsky's father had never talked about his family history. She had to travel to Belarus to learn how her relatives died at the hands of the Nazis. The programme ended with her cousin Bennie chanting a traditional Jewish prayer in the ruins of a synagogue where members of her family had been killed, a deeply moving moment.

Genealogy is our generation's rock and roll. Tap

'ancestry' into any search engine, and you will find infinite ways of working your way back through time. As I followed my intricate pathway through census forms, birth certificates and wills for the programme, I understood so much more about my history, and genetic inheritance. The one warning I would offer is that if there are blanks and silences in your family history, be prepared for any possibility, for we all have more than one skeleton rattling away in the cupboard. So leave well alone, if you only want to hear good news about the past. The effect of my exploration was to create in me an abiding gratitude to the country my ancestors adopted as their own, this gorgeous, democratic, green and pleasant land filled with people who, for all their eccentricities, are courageous and compassionate. I felt then, and feel still, unbelievably lucky. And that is no bad thing. If cultivating our memories, every kind of memory, short-term, long-term, even our own particular race memories, can give us a sense of identity, stimulate our brain cells and lift our spirits, let alone informing our families, that's no small recommend-ation. Maybe it's our duty to the next generation to explore and record our memories, to give them a sense of their own history. What's more, it's fun. As J. M. Barrie said, 'God gave us memory so that we might have roses in December.' With such a precious gift at our disposal, I think you may find, as I have, that roses in December become your favourite flowers.

The Moral of the Story . . .

> *To be seventy years young is sometimes far more cheerful and hopeful than to be forty years old*

Oliver Wendell Holmes

A year ago, travelling with a group around the extraordinary archaeological sites in Libya, I met an impeccably dressed man I'll call Charles, because that is not his name. I spotted him standing on a hill looking around the Roman city of Leptis Magna, staring across to a far away range of pillars. He reminded me a little of my father, he had the same rather sweet, abstracted. expression of someone whose gaze rarely focuses on the here and now, because he is more used to thinking of time, space and mathematics. Which my father was, and which, I soon discovered, Charles was too, because he was a physicist. Unlike my father, Charles was extremely rich. That fact emerged slowly through our conversations, because he was shamefaced about it. He had made some kind of discovery some years back which he was able to patent, and which was being manufactured under licence, so money was pouring into his bank accounts, while he was free to enjoy spending it. Charles was shy. He seemed reluctant to join the rest of the group at the end of the day, which was sad, because I suspected he was lonely, and that he would have been good company. He'd had an interesting life, he had a gleam in his eyes, and he evidently took great care about his appearance. His grey receding hair was brushed neatly back, his pastel shirts and chinos were well cut, looked expensive and were always beautifully laundered and ironed. He was slim, and clearly had been sporty, indeed he still was fit and spry, as he clambered easily over and around the various classical cities we were exploring in Libya. One afternoon, as we sat under the arches of a Roman temple listening to the rush and scrabble of the sea, I started to ask Charles about himself, and to my surprise he talked quite frankly. It turned out that he wasn't lonely at all. 'I have a partner at home in Hampshire,' he told me. 'Anne's just turned forty, very attractive, she's a musician. We get on well together.'

'Is she single?'

'Oh yes, she's divorced. I've known her about a year.'

'How did you meet?'

'At a local riding stables. It all started when we rode out together. I have a neighbour who looks after me, and when she realised Anne and I were getting on so well, she said I should ask her out to dinner. I said I couldn't possibly. She said why not? Anne could always turn me down if she wanted to. So I did. And she accepted. We went out several times and we got on better and better. So when I decided to go on a riding holiday to Scotland for a week, my neighbour asked me why I didn't invite Anne to join me. I was worried, of course, because that was a much bigger step. But in the end I asked her, and she said yes. We had a marvellous week together. Just wonderful. And we've been going out ever since.'

'Why haven't you brought her with you on this trip?'

'It's complicated. I was nervous the people in the group would think she was my daughter. She's very attractive.'

That didn't quite make sense to me. 'You could have explained . . .'

'I know. But she thinks I'm sixty-five.'

'And?'

'I'm eighty.'

I took a startled breath. He certainly didn't look eighty. Or at least he didn't look a traditional eighty. But eighty is, after all, the new sixty. I asked Charles what his family think of the relationship.

'My brother thinks she's a gold digger,' he told me with an amused gleam in his eye. 'I say fine, in that case let her keep on digging. I'm having fun.'

'Does she take advantage of you, do you give her loads of presents?'

'One or two. Nothing ridiculous.'

'Like?'

'We go to the ballet, she loves to and so do I. So I bought her a red velvet evening dress to wear for a gala performance. And some diamond earrings.'

It was beginning to sound a little like *Pretty Woman*. How was it going to end? It occurred to me that perhaps one reason he hadn't brought her on the North African trip was that if she caught sight of his passport his secret would be revealed. But would that really be such a disaster?

He shook his head. 'The trouble is that if she knew I'm eighty, she might not think I'm a very good long-term prospect. Which I suppose I'm not.'

To me, Charles looked as if he had at least twenty years ahead of him.

'In any case,' I said, 'no one's guaranteed another ten years. In five minutes we could all be crushed by a falling brick.'

We both looked up, where an enormous block of black granite was balanced on an architrave over our heads. He smiled. 'I know. And right now the fantastic thing is the fun we have together. We play golf, we ride, we sail. And when we're together we just chat away, and laugh.'

And make love, I had no doubt, but I didn't say so.

So were his family right, to fear that Anne was perfectly well aware of his real age, but was humouring him for the sake of his money, the red velvet dress, the diamond earrings? Who was exploiting whom? And did it really matter?

From Anne's point of view, as the proverb says, it's better to be an old man's darling than a young man's slave, and she'd already had one bad relationship, so why not enjoy this one while it lasted? From Charles's point of view, giving clearly gave him pleasure. A birth certificate is hardly a sacred piece of paper, and there is no eleventh commandment, thou shalt not marry someone forty years your junior.

It occurred to me that Charles's story summed up the most objectionable side of ageism. Until we started to count the four decades built up in the age-gap between them, all that mattered was that Anne and he talked so well together, laughed so much, and enjoyed their love-making and their life. The first thing I had noticed about Charles was his smart appearance, now I realised it was a measure of his high self-esteem, and what I had thought was shyness was, in reality, independence. Perhaps Anne, too, had a sheen on her, caused by the knowledge that she was loved and prized. Who were his family and I, after all, to disapprove of their relationship simply on the grounds of his age?

In a sense, their story encapsulates the problem we all face, we who are used to carving our own paths through the world, and who now resent being pigeon-holed by our sell-by date. Why, after all, should we be governed by a date-stamp, when some people are old at seventeen, and others are young at ninety? Maybe in the past the older generation clung on to power too long, and ambitious young people were denied the opportunities their talent deserved because of the log-jam of geriatric dictators in their way. That was quite wrong. But it is just as wrong now to 'top slice', and throw out valuable staff who still have a great deal to contribute.

Charles needed a hefty nudge from his neighbour before he dared ask Anne out to dinner. He knew he was risking rejection, but in the end he achieved what most he wanted, a new relationship. Admittedly it was a gamble, and I suppose it could still end in tears. As the story of Heather Mills and Paul McCartney proves, love in the third age may carry a heavy price tag. But I suspect that Charles would argue that for him, the fun would be worth the cost, and maybe we could learn from him. Perhaps we all need that little extra spur to bring our dreams a bit closer, to summon up enough courage to seek a new partner, apply for a university course, sell the old house, become a charity volunteer, ride bareback round the world, grab whatever new experience we hanker after, to add sparkle and substance to our memories.

If you are hesitating on the brink, I do hope some of the thoughts in this book will give you just the little push you need. With dreams within our grasp, it would be a shame to have nothing but a collection of regrets instead. Several years ago a friend said to me, 'Never forget this isn't a dress rehearsal', and that comment made me rethink myself and my life. So this is where my thesis ends, and your life takes over. The next pages will depend on you, but don't wait too long before you make up your mind what new pastures you want to explore. As Rabbi Hillel said two thousand years ago: 'If I am not for myself, then who will be? If I am only for myself, then what am I? And if not now, when?'

And Finally . . .

There are two ways ahead. One is to close the book, make a cup of tea, and carry on regardless. The other is to ask yourself the following questions because, who knows, it could change your life!

In the average day, what stolen pleasure would I most like to repeat more often?

What part of the country, or the world, have I always wanted to explore, but never had the time?

What ten pieces of music would I like to have constant access to on an iPod?

Which three old friends do I keep meaning to have lunch with?

What DVD of a film or a TV show invariably makes me smile, even when I'm gloomy? Do I possess a copy, and do I know exactly where it is?

What is my favourite food treat? When did I last have it?

When did I last give a party?

When did I last stand on my head?

When did I last dance, either alone or in company, to one of the favourite songs of my youth?

Is there someone in my life I really love, but keep forgetting to say so?

What one skill have I always longed to acquire?

What is my favourite charity? Do they need my help?

When did I last do a crossword or a sudoku?

When did I last have a massage?

When did I last make a new friend?

What's the last new word I learned?

Have I put together a memory box, with favourite words and pictures in it, to leave to those I will leave behind? And have I made a will, and left instructions for my own funeral?

When did I last take a bath by candlelight, or a swim by moonlight?

When did I last have a hug?

Looking back over the last fifty New Year's Eves, which one did I most enjoy and why? Can I do that again this year?

Is there a picture I particularly love, and do I have a copy where I can see it whenever I wish?

When and where was I happiest? Can I recapture that memory whenever I wish?

Can I spare £5, or £10, or £25, and is there someone, or some cause, who would appreciate it, if I donated it as a motiveless gift?

When did I last pay a friend, or a stranger, a compliment?

If I met myself aged seventeen, what would most thrill and surprise my teenage self about the way my life has turned out?

What am I most looking forward to?

And having answered all that, isn't it time to give myself a treat?

If not now . . .

Index

Warning

When I am an old woman I shall wear purple
With a red hat which doesn't go, and doesn't suit me.
And I shall spend my pension on brandy and summer gloves
And satin sandals, and say we've no money for butter.
I shall sit down on the pavement when I'm tired
And gobble up samples in shops and press alarm bells
And run my stick along the public railings
And make up for the sobriety of my youth.
I shall go out in my slippers in the rain
And pick the flowers in other people's gardens
And learn to spit.

You can wear terrible shirts and grow more fat
And eat three pounds of sausages at a go
Or only bread and pickle for a week
And hoard pens and pencils and beermats and things in boxes.

But now we must have clothes that keep us dry
And pay our rent and not swear in the street
And set a good example for the children.
We must have friends to dinner and read the papers.

But maybe I ought to practise a little now?
So people who know me are not too shocked and surprised
When suddenly I am old, and start to wear purple.

Jenny Joseph